2001

VAN GOGH

VAN GOGH

William Feaver

PORTLAND HOUSE

NEW YORK

First published 1990 by Studio Editions Ltd.
Princess House, 50 Eastcastle Street
London W1N 7AP, England

This edition published 1990 by Portland House
a division of dithilium Press Ltd.
Distributed by Crown Publishers, Inc.
225 Park Avenue South
New York, New York 10003

ISBN 0-517-67957-4

Printed and bound in Italy

h g f e d c b a

'Well, the truth is, we can only make our pictures speak':
Vincent Van Gogh: letter to his brother
Theo. c.27 July 1890.

INTRODUCTION

'Through the tops of the trees one could see that part . . . which lies on the hill; the houses with their red roofs, uncurtained windows and green gardens; and the grey spire high above them; and below, the long grey bridge with the tall poplars on either side, over which the people passed like little black figures.'

This could almost be Auvers-sur-Oise, where Van Gogh stayed as Dr Gachet's patient for the last months of his life. Or somewhere near Saint-Rémy, where houses gaped by the roadside and trees were so torn between ground and sky. It is a sort of picture-book view, boldly coloured, obviously simplified, the little black figures adding animation. It was in fact Richmond-on-Thames.

Vincent Van Gogh saw there what he chose to see, a setting in which he felt he could serve and thrive. It wasn't so much the actual Richmond, more the ideal place where, one bright Sunday in November 1876, he was about to preach his first sermon.

Some months earlier he had been greatly impressed by George Eliot's novel *Felix Holt*, so much so that he had sent his brother Theo a copy, urging him to read it and pass it on to their parents. Holt, 'a rough, severe fellow', as he described himself, dedicated his life to serving the poor. 'Preaching is your only vocation', says Esther to Felix. 'A woman doesn't like a man who tells her the truth.' She eventually marries him. Years later Van Gogh was to remark that his painting *Vincent's Bedroom in Arles* was inspired by the character of Felix Holt, by the whole tone of the book.

'Yet there were the grey steeples too, and the church-yards, with their grassy mounds and venerable head-stones, sleeping in the sunlight', Eliot wrote. 'In those midland districts the traveller passed rapidly from one phase of English life to another: after looking down on a village dingy with coal-dust, noisy with the shaking of looms, he might skirt a parish all of fields, high hedges and deep-rutted lanes.'

When Van Gogh preached his first sermon he had at the back of his mind 'a delightful thought that in the future wherever I go, I shall preach the Gospel.' In essence this was true. While ceasing to be Dutch Reformed or Methodist or even Christian at all in a conventional sense, he always held to his gospel of dogged ardour. This is what makes his art uniquely direct.

Like Felix Holt he passed rapidly from one phase of life to another. Unlike other painters, he was always the amateur preacher, strong to save. His ideal artist was one who 'lived serenely as a greater artist than all other artists, designing marble and clay as well as colour, working in living flesh'. Christ was that artist; and Felix Holt the radical was Christ-like, renouncing all for 'a very bare and simple life'.

In the autumn of 1876 Van Gogh was still the ex-trainee art dealer, the schoolteacher turned evangelist with no idea of becoming an artist. Richmond as he described it (in reality one of the most respectable London suburbs) was a Symbolist composition prefiguring Gauguin's Pont-Aven, a Biblical town on a hill where, he hoped, miracles would happen.

'To do this *well*, one must have the gospel in one's heart', he wrote to Theo. As one son of Pastor Theodorus Van Gogh to another, he had no need to stress the importance of the sermon in a week's work, the God-given opportunity to berate, explain, inspire. 'When I was

Self-Portrait, December 1887.

The Yellow House in Arles, September 1888.

standing in the pulpit, I felt like somebody who, emerging from a dark cave below ground, returns to the light of day.'

He preached in English, naturally, and his words must have struck his Methodist congregation as strange, uncouth perhaps, but blatantly sincere.

'It is a good belief that our life is a pilgrim's progress – that we are strangers on the earth . . . our life is a long walk or journey from earth to Heaven.'

He warmed to his theme, repeating himself in order to impress upon the Richmond Methodists (and upon his brother to whom he sent the sermon, written out from memory) the full meaning, as he saw it, of his text: Psalm 119, verse 19: 'I am a stranger on earth, hide not Thy commandments from me.'

'Our life is a pilgrim's progress. *I once saw a very beautiful picture*: it was a landscape at evening. In the distance on the right hand side a row of hills appearing blue in the evening mist. Above those hills the splendour of the sunset, the grey clouds with their linings of silver and gold and purple . . . Through the landscape a road leads to a high mountain far, far away; on the top of that mountain is a city whereon the setting sun casts a glory.

'On the road walks a pilgrim, staff in hand. He has been walking for a good long while already and he is very tired. And now he meets a woman, or figure in black, that makes one think of St Paul's words: *"As being sorrowful yet always rejoicing"* . . .'

Van Gogh's description, coloured by his enthusiasm, was of a painting by George Boughton, *God Speed*!, exhibited two years before at the Royal Academy Exhibition. The painting was a large, prosaic study of 'Pilgrims

setting out for Canterbury: time of Chaucer'. In his mind's eye Van Gogh conflated the Chaucerian and the Bunyanesque. He transformed Richmond into a Jerusalem.

Twelve years later, at the start of what he called his 'campaign in the South', he said: 'The only choice I have is between being a good painter and a bad one.' His was a moral aesthetic. Good painting blazed with certainty and lingered in the memory. Bad paintings were muddled. In that 'different light' of Provence, where what he had once regarded as the 'healthy colours' of the North were replaced by 'sky blue, orange, pink, vermilion, bright yellow, bright green, bright wine-red, violet', he came to a

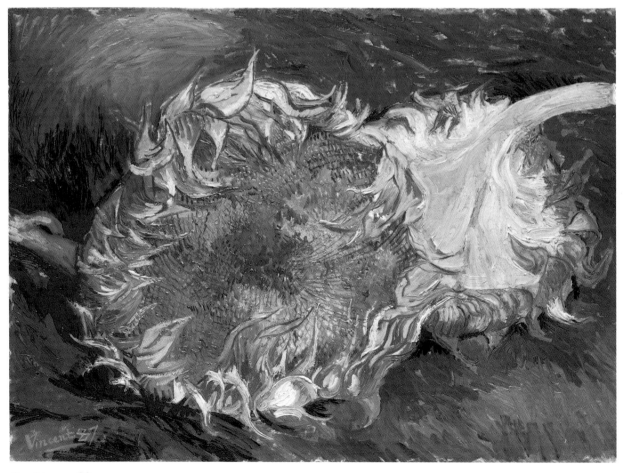

Sunflowers, 1887.

Dance Hall with Dancing Women, November 1885.

new perception of the redeeming powers of colour. In the asylum at Saint-Rémy he made coloured versions of engravings after Doré, Delacroix, Rembrandt and Millet, adding sunshine, gold, warmth, ethereality to scenes of exhaustion, grief and dumb endurance.

Van Gogh the preacher, inspired by the graphic journalists of the London illustrated papers, 'their Monday-morning-like soberness and studied simplicity and solemnity and keen analysis', turned into Van Gogh the colourist to whom nothing seemed more peaceful than yellow and blue, nothing more indicative of 'the powers of darkness' than malachite green, sulphur and red. He moved from text and illustration to a language that struck him as universal: the colours of sun, sunflowers, colours for all seasons, colours with symbolic meanings but direct impact.

He was 23 when he delivered his first sermon. He was to spend about five years obsessed with Bible study, evangelism, work among the poor of the Borinage in Belgium and experiencing failure. 'But I'm proof against

Gas Tanks near the Hague, 1882.

Wheatfield with Sheaves and Windmill, August 1885.

that word failure', said George Eliot's Felix Holt. 'The only failure a man ought to fear is failure in cleaving to the purpose he sees to be best.' Turning to drawing, gradually clarifying his ideas about art, he reassured himself that the act of delineation is in its way redemptive. All things become simply crayon or ink on paper. 'If one draws a willow as if it were a living being – and after all, it really is – then the surroundings follow in due course if one has concentrated all one's attention only on that same tree, not giving up until one has put some life into it.'

Van Gogh's career as preacher-turned-artist lasted ten years. For more than half that time he trained himself and translated his ideas, uncertain as to where they would lead him. By 1883 he was convinced he knew his way. 'I have found in my work something which I can devote myself to heart and soul, and which inspires me and gives a meaning to life,' he wrote to Theo. 'I have a firm *faith* in art, a firm confidence in its being a powerful stream which carries a man to a harbour.'

The pilgrim progressed. The appeal of his faith in art lay in its demands: constant practice, perpetual endeavour to be truthful. But he took with him, from Sunday school teaching into art, certain assumptions. He took the most blatant images of death-in-life, of growth, fulfilment, of harvest and renewal, and presented them whole. Each field, each tree, each person confronted for portrait purposes signified an attempt to grasp essentials. The presence of the pair of boots, the sunflowers, the nests and baskets, the stalwart chair, the village cowering with rain striking down, was both illustrative and illuminating.

'It was a clear autumn day and a beautiful walk from here to Richmond along the Thames' he wrote to Theo, describing how the day he preached his 'God Speed!' sermon had gone. That afternoon, while still only an occasional sketcher, Van Gogh the artist began.

Through Van Gogh's eyes, through his impassioned speed (particularly in his last months), through his lavish use of 'sky blue, orange, pink, vermilion, bright yellow, bright green, bright wine-red, violet', through his letters and through his expository zeal, an unprecedented sort of painting came about. To reach into the hearts of his congregation young Van Gogh resorted to ringing quotations and straightforward, confessional appeals. In his paintings he eventually did the same, moving from scenes of labour and hardship, such as he had seen from time to time in *The Graphic*, to images that had moral presence. The subject matter was not, in itself, remarkable. At the 1874 Royal Academy, in Goupil's, in The Hague, he found plenty to impress him. At the Paris Salon, in the Luxembourg gallery too, he saw paintings of the humble peasant, the daily task, shepherding, husbandry, the small pleasures of simple lives and the long dullness of grief. His versions of such art were often shocking because they were so unrefined, so lacking in finesse. In other words, Van Gogh went beyond Millet – who never neglected to show that he was, after all, highly skilled, however lowly his motifs – by becoming so direct a painter.

Starry Night, painted in June 1889: 'The olives with white cloud and background of mountains, as well as the rising moon and *the impression of night*, are exaggerations from the point of view of arrangement, the lines being distorted like those in old woodcuts.' Starting with the plain statements and glaring verdicts of English picture-journalism as his guide, Van Gogh developed an instinct for the ground swell and the rising sap. The weightiness of his stooping miners, the women bent under sacks of coal, the vigour of the wheat stooks, the rhythmic thump of women taking to the floor in the Antwerp dance hall, show him quickening in response. The paintings of nests and baskets, potatoes, a skull and Père Tanguy seated like

Carpenter's Yard and Laundry, 1882.

a down-to-earth Buddha against a backdrop of sketchy Japanese prints, reveal his self-taught ability to do without the correctitude of the fully-trained. Suddenly, unhesitatingly, he puts life into them.

Van Gogh retained his humility. He remained convinced, to the end, that he was a lesser artist than Gauguin, not least because Gauguin told him so. It was the humility of the former preacher (rather than, in Gauguin's case, the former stockbroker) and it meant that copying was more than a useful exercise. It was a form of recitation or restatement. The aim in art was to achieve the repeatability of a well-known, well-loved poem. In his sermon to the Richmond Methodists he recited part of Christina Rossetti's 'Up-hill':

Does the road wind up-hill all the way?
Yes, to the very end.
Will the day's journey take the whole long day?
From morn to night, my friend.

The graphic artists he admired – artists like Hubert Herkomer and Luke Fildes – were famous for the immediacy of their illustration and reportage. Fildes draw Charles Dickens' study at Gad's Hill the morning after his death: the place where *The Mystery of Edwin Drood* was never to be resolved, where the author's chair was left empty. Van Gogh had that image in his thoughts when he painted his own rough, severe chair, and Gauguin's more elaborate one, in the Yellow House in Arles.

Fildes went on to become one of the most popular late nineteenth-century painters in England and America, largely on the strength of one painting, of which a photogravure, published in 1892, sold phenomenal numbers of copies. *The Doctor*, commissioned in 1887 and exhibited at the Royal Academy in 1891, was – unknown to Van Gogh – the last and greatest of what might be termed the Felix Holt genre. The doctor attends the sickbed, possibly the deathbed, of a child. The bed is

The Chair, 1890.

improvised, on two chairs. The doctor sits, waiting. The emblems of sickness – medicine bottle, jug, lamp still burning as dawn comes, bird in cage, and the child's own small chair already empty, are all around. This picture, composed with immense care, painted in a specially built mock-up cottage, was worked on, start to finish, during the years in which Van Gogh moved from Paris to Arles, to Saint-Rémy and, finally, to Auvers.

The difference between one, high resolution, studio-based bid for universal sympathy and all those other paintings Van Gogh produced in that time, is more than

The Potato Eaters, 1885.

strikingly coincidental. It marks the distance that grew between Van Gogh's literary inspired ideas and his directly inspired painting. *The Potato Eaters* of 1885, based on studies of the De Groot family, is the closest he got to the set-piece methods of *The Doctor*. Moving away from the North, first to Paris and then to the Midi, meant that he lost contact with that sort of tableau painting. Those he met in Paris, notably Pissarro, stimulated him to impatience with such exhaustively plotted motifs. He learnt to rely not on a dramatist's chiaroscuro but on the vibrancy and power of colour.

'By intensifying *all* the colours one arrives once again at quietude and harmony.'

15

At the end of Zola's *L'Œuvre*, a novel Van Gogh read soon after it was published in 1886, the painter Claude Lantier (a character part Manet, part Cézanne, as Zola saw them) commits suicide and is buried in Avenue 3 of a 'vast flat cemetery, still quite new', where the priest's '*Revertitur in terram suam unde erat*' is drowned by the snorts of a shunting engine, on the embankment overlooking the cemetery.

'It had rained so heavily during the past few days, and the earth was so very soft, that one side of the grave suddenly fell in and one of the grave-diggers had to jump down and clear it with his spade; which he did with slow rhythmic gestures that seemed likely to go on for ever, greatly to the annoyance of the priest ... Up on the embankment the railway engine was in action again, backing and blasting out showers of red-hot cinders into the dull grey sky.'

Van Gogh's paintings often serve as descriptions. There are railways bringing modernity to the timeless rural scene. There are odd juxtapositions: the harvest fields rolling towards the horizontal billows of steam from the passing train. In Zola and Maupassant, Van Gogh found the telling contrasts he loved, the constant signs of wider or darker possibilities behind ordinary appearances.

Zola's *Germinal*, the mining community drama set – in effect – in Van Gogh's Borinage, is in black and grey relieved only by the warmth of family and friendships, and by the torch of goodness, the small beacons of self-sacrifice. The factual side of Zola related him to the *Graphic* artists. His other aspect, his virtuosity, was more Manet, more Frans Hals.

As far as Van Gogh was concerned, Frans Hals was admirable not just because his technique was so vivid ('hands that lived, but were not finished in the sense they demand nowadays') but because he concentrated so.

Women Carrying Coal, autumn 1882.

Mlle Gachet in her Garden, June 1890.

'He never painted Christs, annunciations to the shepherds, angels, crucifixions or resurrections; he never painted nude, voluptuous and bestial women.

'He did portraits, and nothing, nothing else.'

Writing to Emile Bernard (the painter he felt closest to in terms of Symbolism), Van Gogh insisted that Hals alone of the Dutch masters knew not only how to paint ('no less than twenty-seven blacks') but what was right to paint.

'It is as beautiful as Zola, healthier as well as merrier, but as true to life, because his epoch was healthier and less dismal.'

When Van Gogh left Paris for Arles he went in hopes of finding a healthier life, away from the pressures that were turning him into an alcoholic, away from distracting artists with their competitive instincts. He went to find suitable locations and worthwhile sitters.

Virtually the first person he met in Arles was Joseph Roulin the station postal official. He sat for Van Gogh, for something to do. ('He lives a great deal in cafés and is certainly more or less a drinker . . . but he is so much the reverse of a sot, his exaltation is so natural, so intelligent and he argues with such sweep.'). Roulin was a Hals figure, and Van Gogh painted him as such. Where Hals had satin and ruffs to deal with, Van Gogh had the rough serge and the peaked cap. He set Roulin in a chair, the inveterate Republican prepared to argue. He put him against wallpaper, his beard as luxuriant as the patterning. He painted the whole Roulin family, one by one.

'What appeals to me most . . . is the portrait, the modern portrait.'

Joseph Roulin, Armand Roulin, Camille Roulin, Madame Augustine Roulin (*La Berceuse*) and baby Marcelle Roulin were all that he had hoped for. He idealized them, describing to Emile Bernard the affection Joseph felt for the baby, his tenderness and consideration. Roulin helped him after the crisis of December 1888 when he had his breakdown. The Roulins were a nestful of characters. When he couldn't paint them, or others such as Lieutenant Milliet, the Zouave, or the doctor at Arles hospital or his doctor and warder at Saint-Rémy, Dr Gachet and Dr Gachet's daughter, he had to paint himself. When that palled, and weather allowed, he went out to paint the countryside instead. Or there were the various forms of still-life: the table-top arrangement, the flowers, the vegetables available.

'I think a great lesson taught by the old Dutch masters is the following: to consider drawing and colour one.'

In Antwerp he had observed how Rubens drew the lines in his faces 'with streaks of pure red'. The energy of

Portrait of the Artist's Mother, October 1888.

Hals, he noted, lay in the darting, tweaking brush-strokes. Painting lemons or potatoes, he drew outlines and shadowing in lemon yellow and dirty ochres. He learnt to exaggerate, to see places as spiritually golden or scarlet or sulphurous, and to colour them as such.

In Paris, seeing how Pissarro dabbed and Seurat flecked, he had been conscious of being the Northerner learning to paint lightly. In Arles he was the lone explorer, not so much the missionary as the venturesome topographer annexing the territory – and a few of the locals –

Portrait of Dr Rey, January 1889.

Self-Portrait, March 1887.

Red Vineyards at Arles, 1888.

for his purposes. The 'campaign in the South' was an overnight journey in the general direction of the exotic. It wasn't Japan, but it was more Japanese than Neunen.

Arriving, to find snow, he reminded himself of views of Mount Fuji and Japanese back yards with the cane fences and cherry trees framing every vista. Japan, known to him through prints and hearsay, represented harmony. There, he believed, peasants and artists fitted effortlessly together into the scheme of things. The land was the

perfect backdrop. Art was everyday. The prints that served as wrapping paper were images of a society in which the artist's calling was similar to that of a monk. If the Dutch masters had taught him to treat colour and line as one, the Japanese implied, for him, an even more complete aesthetic: one of dramatic cohesion. Abrupt close-ups and landscapes snowy blank or sliced with rain superimposed themselves on the faces he studied and the fields he walked through. Out on the road to Tarascon,

The Dance Hall at Arles, December 1888.

passing among the smallholdings of the Crau, he translated as he went. Spring turned into summer, the corn grew; the maddening Mistral sharpened the light, scouring as it blew, making a day's work outdoors difficult if not impossible.

As Van Gogh learnt the vocabulary of the Crau, drawing it with a reed pen, devising a shorthand for fence and irises, rocks and stubble, he became confident as never before. Here at last was a stretch of land that (although it reminded him of de Koninck, the Dutch master of horizontality) he could declare his. Through the summer of 1888 he annexed what suited him, from Montmajor to Les Saintes-Maries-de-la-Mer, painting as fast as he could in order to seize hold. 'Quick souls', George Eliot says in *Felix Holt*, 'have their intensest life in the first anticipatory sketch of what may or will be.'

'*Admire* as much as you can; *most people do not admire enough*' was Van Gogh's advice to his brother in 1874. Admiration lay behind the curious opposites in his style. There were the Japanese prints, admired because they seemed to represent a perfect, stylistic solution to social problems. There were the crusty, turgid paintings of Monticelli: 'What a mistake the Parisians make in not having a palate for crude things, for Monticellis, for common earthenware.' Gauguin (admired for his forcefulness by Van Gogh) despised thick paint, and the idea that 'common earthenware', or its painterly equivalent, should be appreciated on clumsy moral grounds. But then most of Van Gogh's ideas ('I can't help liking Meissoniers') were based on early loyalties and obstinate likings. They were shaped in isolation.

Van Gogh's Symbolism (the enlarged sun, the nest woven onto the branch, the billowing wheat-field enclosed by a wall) was inspired more by the metaphors of the Psalms than by other art. Yet, as an almost entirely self-taught painter, and as a draughtsman who had failed every test, by Antwerp Academy criteria, he longed for a common language in which he would (trilingual as he already was) be fluent.

'More and more it seems to me that the pictures which must be made so that painting should be wholly itself, and should raise itself to a height equivalent to the serene summits which the Greek sculptors, the German musicians, the writers of French novels reached, are beyond the power of an isolated individual; so they will probably be created by groups of men combining to execute an idea held in common.'

Style would reconcile. Style would be attuned to overwhelming impulse. Wagnerian, so to speak. ('What an artist . . . one like that in painting would be something. *It will come.*'). Gauguin and he would begin an artists' settlement in Arles. The Yellow House would become an outpost of the new serenity, a solar cell, a spiritual abode.

'Painting ought to be done at the public expense, instead of the artists being overburdened with it', he wrote to Theo in August 1888. Van Gogh's painting, of course, was done at his brother's expense. Money for subsistence, tubes of paint in sufficient quantity for him to paint quicker than Monticelli but just as thickly, were the essential accompaniment to Theo's replies to Vincent's letters. The relationship of the brothers was, theoretically, that of artist and dealer. The Van Goghs were eminent over two generations in the Netherlands, as important figures in the art trade. Vincent's failure as a dealer and his re-emergence, after the wilderness years of evangelism, as the family artist (in succession to Anton Mauve, related to his mother by marriage) could be rationalized as a false start followed by long-term investment in his talent. But Theo's support was, as they both knew, far more than that. Theo arranged Gauguin's move to Arles; Theo listened; Theo allowed himself to become the recipient of Vincent's outpourings.

'My work is my body and soul, and for it, I risk my life and my reason.'

The letters Van Gogh wrote, to his mother and sister, to Bernard and Gauguin and most of all – more than 650 of them – to Theo, turn the paintings into illustrations. Without their running commentary the dates would be uncertain and the intentions would be, more often than not, unstated. The letters exist because Van Gogh moved from home, from the Netherlands and, eventually from Paris. They throw his beginnings as an artist, and his final years into unique focus. Where Delacroix's journals are relatively chatty, Van Gogh's letters address themselves to constant emergencies. They also have something of the confessional tirelessness of the journals that ended on June 22nd 1846:

Garden in Provence, July 1888.

Memories of the North, 1889.

Street in Auvers, 1890.

'God forgive me. Amen
Finis
of
B.R. Haydon
"Stretch me no longer on this rough world" *Lear*
End of Twenty-sixth Volume.'

Haydon, after a lifetime of, as he saw it, unjust neglect by ruling Academicians and art patrons, slit his throat, leaving his journals as a monument to unrequited ambition. Van Gogh's letters are in some ways equivalent to Haydon's eloquent outpourings. They confess his aspirations and list his setbacks. Yet unlike Haydon, Van Gogh had no vanity or self-pity. His letters demanded – and received – response. The solicitude (and francs, paint and canvas) that came by return was vital to him. For although he felt increasingly guilty about imposing on Theo, he could regard his brother as his keeper, his receiver. Theo, in a sense, stood in for posterity and, as he predicted, posterity owes much to Vincent. He said: 'I should not be surprised if my brother were one of the great geniuses and will one day be compared to someone like Beethoven.'

The long conversations-turned-monologues that Vincent held with Theo, writing to him at night, involved descriptions of work accomplished and about to be despatched to Paris, and accounts of what he longed for or planned to do. The letters were substitutes for proper conversations, such as had exhausted Theo when Vincent lived with him in Paris. They reflect his energy, particularly on those days when work went well, days, he reported, when 'the brush-strokes come like clockwork'.

Sometimes such elation was ominous, for Van Gogh worked towards the deadlines of nervous crises. There was panic at the thought of intrusion or change, depression at Christmas. But he also speeded up when the mood seized him, when the irises nodded at him, the fields shivered and the sun brought on the harvest.

A size 30 canvas (roughly 70 by 90 cm.) could be carried easily enough along the road to a chosen spot, and a painting could result in a matter of hours. Tube paints made such rapidity possible. Straight from the tube, often unmixed, his cobalt skies and carmine poppies, raw yellows and greens were the fruits of alacrity. Even when he sat and considered (as in *Night Café* or *Vincent's Bedroom*) the intention remained: to achieve in his rough and ready way what Frans Hals had made to seem spontaneous.

There was a lack of snobbery in Van Gogh's talkative approach. His openness, a goodness verging on naivety that Gauguin especially found intolerable, was the lasting basis of his whole style. No one else would have admitted – in Post-Impressionist circles – to admiring both Meissonier and Monticelli. He painted as he wrote and as he had preached, always in direct speech. He addressed himself to particular subjects ('The cypresses are always occupying my thoughts'), trying them out in words and sketches. 'Cypresses which show off their nightmarish silhouettes of black flame; mountains which rear their backs like mammoths or rhinoceroses.' In his exaltation he echoed the psalmist's 'mountains skipped like rams and the little hills like lambs'.

'Vincent and I simply cannot live together in peace because of incompatability', Gauguin wrote to Theo at the end of the attempt to achieve creative harmony in the Yellow House in Arles. Van Gogh's breakdown, at Christmas 1888, was brought on by Gauguin, by anxiety, perhaps, at Theo's marriage and divided responsibilities, by his remedies ('the only way . . . is to stun myself with a lot of drinking or heavy smoking') and the underlying urgency of painting after painting.

'I am caught in the wheels of the Fine Arts, like wheat

Pollard Willows and Setting Sun, October 1888.

Thatched Cottages in Auvers, July 1890.

between the millstones', he had written to Theo in the summer of 1888. From then onwards he was ground down by the fear of madness. The period in the Arles hospital followed by a whole year at Saint-Rémy (May 1889–May 1890), relieved him of the day-to-day difficulties of providing for himself but the strain of being an inmate aggravated his disorder. He argued to himself that circumstances could be worse. 'By seeing the actual *truth* of the life of these various lunatics and crazy folk I am losing the vague dread, the fear of the thing.'

Painting the view from his upstairs cell, the field seething to the boil, the mountain enlarged and closing in, Van Gogh saw the seasons accelerate, growth one day, stubble the next. 'Life's so short, and especially the number of years in which one's strong enough to risk everything'.

Meadow with Butterflies, May 1890.

The weeks in which he could not work were death to him: blank weeks when Dr Peyron noted 'acute mania with generalized delirium'. Those weeks broke the continuity of nearly ten years. Yet, 'the peasant *must* be a peasant, that digger *must* dig': he revived himself with exercises, making copies from reproductions after Delacroix, Millet and Doré. He added colour and a good-natured burliness to Millet's scenes from peasant life. He

began to consider returning to the homelands of the north.

In his lucid periods ('the unbearable hallucinations have ceased, and are now getting reduced to simple nightmares') he was allowed out, under supervision. He found in the Alpilles a primordial landscape, a path leading into 'Les Peyroulets', a honey-combed, worm-eaten ravine. The convulsive rocks, worn away by the

Entrance to the Public Gardens at Arles, September 1888.

stream, blended with the grey skies of his Netherlands, thatched houses in lumpy villages, places distanced and generalized as he remembered or imagined them.

To go to live in Auvers-sur-Oise for a while was a sensible plan, for there Dr Gachet could keep an eye on him, Theo was within reach, and in the placid North no mistrals blew.

Van Gogh's Auvers period lasted only long enough for him to paint the one season, springtime to high summer, from blossom to reaping. 'The greatest, most powerful imaginations have at the same time made things directly from nature that strike one dumb': in Auvers he studied Daubigny's garden, and painted it, in homage to the painter who had, like Constable, shown that there was nothing too lowly in nature to be worth painting. He painted where Cézanne and Pissarro had been.

Awareness of this did not inhibit him and Auvers soon danced to his rhythm. He moved from church to street to chestnut trees in bloom. He painted Dr Gachet's portrait (describing it to Gauguin as having 'the heart-broken expression of our time') and he moved out into the fields, unaccompanied.

The landscape of the Oise valley was all green and shallow, he found. But there it was and for some weeks (the painter *must* paint) he made the best of it.

Harvest-time again and, for 'the sower of God's word', momentary fulfilment. Two years earlier he had written to Emile Bernard: 'I am still charmed by the magic of hosts of memories of the past, of a longing for the infinite, of which the sower and the sheaf are the symbols.'

Now, even now, he could remember perhaps the circumstances of his first sermon. 'It was a clear autumn day and a beautiful walk from here to Richmond along the Thames, in which the great chestnut trees with their load of yellow leaves and the clear blue sky were mirrored,' he had written to Theo in 1876 as he began.

'On the road walks a pilgrim, staff in hand. He has been walking for a good long while already and he is very tired. And now he meets a woman, or figure in black, that makes one think of St Paul's words: "*As being sorrowful yet always rejoicing*".'

St Paul's Hospital, Saint-Rémy, 1889.

CHRONOLOGY

1852

30 March: Vincent Willem, son of Revd. Theodorus Van Gogh (1822–85) and Anna Carbentus (1819–1906), born dead.

1853

30 March: Vincent Willem Van Gogh born in Groot Zundert, Brabant. Three of his uncles were art dealers.

1857

1 May: Theo Van Gogh born.

1861

Attends village school.

1864–1866

Private boarding school at Zevenbergen. 'It was an autumn day and I stood on the steps of Mr Provily's school and watched as my father and mother drove away.'

1866

September: Attends Willem II Rijks Hogere Burgerschool in Tilburg.

1869

30 July: Becomes assistant in the Hague branch of Paris art dealers Goupil & Co.

1870

November: Father moves to Helvoist.

1872

Begins correspondence with Theo (who is still at school).

1873

May: Transferred by Goupils to their London branch.

August: Lodges at 87 Hackford Road, Stockwell, South London.

1874

June: Holiday with parents at Helvoist. 'Lately I took up drawing again'.

July: Returns to London with sister Anna.

August: Rejected by Eugenie Loyer, his landlady's daughter.

November: Transferred to Goupils in Paris.

December: Holiday with parents.

1875

January: Returns to London.

May: Transferred again to Paris

October: With colleague Harry Gladwell 'the rest of the evening I

read aloud, generally from the Bible. We intend to read it all the way through.'

December: Etten for Christmas. Returns to Paris and is dismissed.

1876

14 April: To Ramsgate in Kent, where he becomes assistant teacher in a school run by William Stokes, 'a ghost always dressed in black'.

June: Walks to Welwyn, north of London, to see his sister Anna, then to Isleworth where Stokes opens a new school in Twickenham Road.

July: Joins Revd. Thomas Slade-Jones' school 'Holme Court', also in Twickenham Road.

5 November: Preaches first sermon at Richmond Methodist Church, Kew Road. Text: 'I am a stranger on the earth, hide not thy commandments from me'.

December: To Etten for Christmas and decides not to return to London. 'Lately it has seemed to me that there are no professions in the world other than those of schoolmaster and clergyman, with all that lies between these two – such as missionary, especially a London missionary.'

1877

January: Working for Dordrecht bookseller: job arranged by his Uncle Vincent.

May: Moves to Amsterdam, studies Greek and Latin for university entrance. Lodges with Uncle Jan (Director of the shipyards), supervised in studies by Uncle Pastor Stricker.

1878

July: Stops studying and moves to theological college at Laeken near Brussels.

November: Fails to qualify. Returns to Etten.

December: Leaves for Borinage in South Belgium to become a temporary preacher in Wasmes. 'You know that one of the fundamental truths not only of the Gospel but of the whole Bible is that light shines in the darkness. Through darkness to light.' During this period went down into mines, sided with strikers. Appointment not renewed.

1879

August: Preacher working on his own at Cuesmes near Mons. Tramps the roads, sleeping in barns. Destitute and estranged from Theo for nine months.

1880

August: Stops missionary work to become an artist. Drawing, supported by an allowance from Theo who had begun working for

Goupils. Copies Millet. Ambition to become 'the illustrator of the people'. 'I cannot tell you how happy I am to have taken up drawing again. I had long been thinking of it.'

October: To Brussels. Enrols at Art Academy

1881

April: Returns to Etten. Row with father over becoming an artist.

August: In love with his cousin Kee Vos, daughter of Pastor Stricker. Rejected.

November: In The Hague. Begins collecting illustrations from *The Graphic* and *Illustrated London News*. Tutored for a while by his cousin by marriage, the Hague School painter Anton Mauve. First paintings: still lives.

December: Quarrels with Mauve.

1882

January: Meets prostitute Sien Hoornik and takes her in. 'When *love* is dead does not *charity* become more alive?' Uncle Cornelius commissions drawings: views of The Hague. Makes a perspective frame 'The lines of roofs and drainpipes recede now like a charm!'

August: Theo provides money for paint and canvas. 'I care less about earning than about deserving.'

1883

September: Leaving Sien behind, goes to Drenthe in the East Netherlands, staying in Hoogeveen and Nieuw Amsterdam. 'I think I can conclude that my body will hold out a few years more, say six to ten . . . I do not intend to spare myself.'

December: Returns to his parents in Nuenen.

In the Orchard, 1883.

1884

Weaver: The Whole Loom, March 1884.

January: Nurses his mother while she is laid up with a broken leg. Involvement with Margot Begeman, one of three sisters living next door. She attempts suicide. Gives lessons to a railway clerk, Van der Wacker, Gestel, son of a painter, and Kerssemakers, a tanner.

The Parsonage Garden in Winter, 1885.

1885

Makes studies of weavers and of the De Groot family in 1884–5. 'If I'm worth something later, I'm worth it now too, for wheat is wheat, though city-dwellers take it first for grass.'

27 March: [Theodorus Van Gogh dies.]

April: *Potato Eaters*.

May: *The Old Tower at Nuenen*.

June: Reads *Germinal* by Zola. 'While trying to go deeper into art, I try at the same time to go deeper into life, for the two go together.' Plans to paint a series of fifty heads. Priest forbids villagers of Nuenen to sit for him.

Two Peasants Working in the Field, April 1885.

October: Three days in Amsterdam, studying especially Frans Hals 'laying on the colour at one touch'. *Still Life with Open Bible*.

27 November: To Antwerp. 'I urgently desire to see Rubens.' Enrols at Art Academy. 'In every city of some importance there is an academy with a choice of models for historical, Arabic, Louis XIV, in short, *all really non-existent figures*.' Fills the walls of his room at 194 rue des Images with Japanese prints acquired in the docks. Infected with syphilis. Loses teeth.

1886

28 February: 'Paris seems as great as the sea.' Arriving in Paris for the first time in ten years he meets Theo, as planned, in the Salon Carré at the Louvre. They live first in the rue Laval, then in a

Bowl of Flowers, 1886.

third-floor apartment at 54 rue Lepic in Montmartre. 'One has a magnificent view of the whole town . . . with the hills of Meudon, St Cloud and so on, on the horizon.'

March–June: Attends Atelier Cormon, where he meets Emile Bernard and Toulouse-Lautrec. Copies antique statuary in the afternoons. Meets Gauguin. 'The air of France clarifies one's ideas and does one good, much good, a world of good.'

May: Eighth (and last) Impressionist exhibition. Includes Pissarro's *View from my Window in Cloudy Weather*, Gauguin's *Bathers*, Signac's *Gasometers, Clichy* and Seurat's *Sunday Afternoon at the Grande Jatte*.

1887

January: Meets Père Tanguy, colour-merchant.

January–March: Arranges two exhibitions at the Café Tambourin: Japanese prints and works by Anquetin, Bernard, Toulouse-Lautrec and himself. Theo writes to his sister: 'The apartment is almost untenable . . . It is as if there were two beings within him, one marvellously gifted, sensitive and tender, the other selfish and hard-hearted . . . what a pity he should be his own enemy.'

May–July: Painting trips, sometimes with Signac, to the suburb of Asnières.

April: Gauguin goes to Martinique, returning sick and penniless in November. Theo succeeds in selling *The Bathers* for him.

Restaurant de la Sirène at Asnières, 1887.

1888

January: Theo buys three paintings from Gauguin who leaves Paris for Pont-Aven. Portrait of Père Tanguy.

February: Encouraged by Lautrec's accounts of the Midi, and following Gauguin's example, leaves Paris. 'If I did not have Theo it would be impossible to achieve with my work what I have to achieve.'

21 February: Arrives in Arles. 'I feel I am in Japan.' Takes room in hotel near the station: Café de l'Alcazar, Place Lamartine.

Wheatfield with Lark, June 1887.

March: Writes to Gauguin suggesting an association of painters. Two landscapes in Salon des Indépendents.

May: Taken two rooms in the 'Yellow House'. No furniture, so uses it only to paint in. Asks Gauguin to come and work with him. Friendship with Lieut. Milliet; they go on sketching excursions.

11–25 June: Trip to Les Saintes-Maries-de-la-Mer. 'The Mediterranean has the colours of mackerel, changeable I mean.' 'Now that I have seen the sea here I am absolutely convinced of the importance of staying in the Midi, and of absolutely piling on, exaggerating the colour – Africa not so far away.'

Seascape at Sainte-Marie, June 1888.

June: *The Sower.* 'I have been longing to do a sower for such a long time . . .' 'A week's hard, close work among the cornfields in the full sun.'

11 August: 'Glorious strong windless heat here.' 'What I learnt in Paris is leaving me, and I am returning to the ideas I had at home before I knew the Impressionists.'

September: With money from a legacy left to Theo, buys chairs and so on for the Yellow House. 'I am thinking of decorating my studio with half-a-dozen pictures of sunflowers.'

17 September: Moves into Yellow House. 'I should like to paint in so simple a way that anyone with eyes can see clearly what is meant.' *Vincent's Bedroom at Arles* (first version).

Boats with Men Unloading Sand, August 1888.

23 October: Gauguin arrives in Arles. He writes: 'Vincent sees this place in terms of Daumier; I see it however as Puvis de Chavannes with colour added . . . He is a romantic while I am rather inclined to a primitive state.'

Mid-December: Trip to Montpellier with Gauguin. Theo tells Vincent about his engagement to Johanna Bonger. *Vincent's Chair, Gauguin's Chair.*

23 December: Mutilates his left ear, following row with Gauguin and takes the lobe to Rachel in 'Maison de Tolerance 1'. Joseph Roulin helps him home. Police send him to the hospital 'Hôtel-Dieu'. Gauguin is arrested, but released almost immediately.

25 December: Theo arrives, summoned by a telegram from Gauguin who leaves with him a day or two later.

1889

7 January: Allowed home, though has to return to the hospital daily to have the wound dressed.

22 January: Roulin is transferred to Marseilles. Paints several versions of his portrait of Madame Roulin, *La Berceuse*. 'It's like a colour lithograph from a cheap shop.'

5 February: Another collapse.

February–March: Petition to have him locked away in the hospital gets thirty signatures.

19 March: Confined to hospital.

23 March: Visit from Signac.

April: Visit from Roulin. Doctor Rey secures him new lodgings.

17 April: Theo and Jo Bonger marrry. Talks of suicide, joining the Foreign Legion, or of being placed in an asylum. 'There I think of accepting outright my calling as a madman, just as Degas took to the guise of a notary.'

30 April: (to his sister Wil) 'In all I have had four great crises, in which I did not know in the least what I said, what I wanted, or what I was doing . . .' *The Crau with Peach Trees in Bloom.*

8 May: Moves to asylum of Saint Paul de Mausole at Saint-Rémy, escorted by Pastor Salles. Admitted as 'third-class inmate', to 'prevent a recurrence of previous attacks'.

Binding the Sheaves, 1889.

June: *Mountain Landscape Seen across the Walls with Rising Sun*. Asks for Works of Shakespeare (Dick's Shilling Edition). 'It is not a return to the romantic, or to religious ideas, no'. *Starry Night*. 'In the blue depths the stars were sparkling, greenish, yellow, white, pink, more brilliant, more sparklingly gemlike than at home – even in Paris.'

5 July: Jo writes to tell him she is pregnant.

6 July: Goes to Arles to collect and send off to Theo paintings left in the Yellow House. Sees Rachel. While returning to Saint-Rémy becomes delirious.

10 July: Another crisis: unable to paint until the end of August. 'I feel a fool having to ask a doctor's permission to paint some pictures.'

September: Starts planning to return North. 'It is hard to leave a place before having proved in some way that one has felt and loved it.'

November: Two days in Arles. *The Ravine*.

December: Breakdown, associated again with Christmas.

1890

January: Breakdown. 'Les Isolés': article by Albert Aurier, Symbolist poet, about Van Gogh, appears in *Mercure de France*.

31 January: Birth of Vincent Willem Van Gogh, to Theo and Jo.

February: Breakdown. Tells his mother he is longing to return to the North. *Branches of an Almond Tree in Blossom*, painted for his nephew. 'A picture for him to hang in their bedroom.' Two months of inaction. 'I am sad and troubled more than I could put into words, and I am just all at sea.'

March: *Red Vines* is sold for 400 francs at the exhibition of 'Les XX' in Brussels.

16 May: Leaves Saint-Rémy after more than a fortnight of rapid and brilliant work. 'I feel so sorrowful at leaving like this that sorrow will be stronger than madness.' In all Van Gogh completed 150 paintings and 100 drawings at Saint-Rémy. 'It did me good going to the South the better to see the North.'

17 May: Arrives in Paris. Stays with Theo, meeting Jo for the first time. Sees Père Tanguy and others and looks through his accumulated work. 'It was odd seeing all my canvases again from the beginning.'

20 May: Goes to Auvers-sur-Oise. Takes a room above the Café Ravoux in the Place de la Mairie. Another room set aside for him to paint in. Meets Dr Gachet. 'He is as disorganized about his job as a doctor as I am about my paintings.' *The Church in Auvers*. 'My health is good, I go to bed at 9 o'clock, but get up at five most of the time . . . I feel much surer of my brush than before going to Arles.' *Portrait of Doctor Gachet* (two versions). 'I feel that I can not do a bad painting every time I go to his house, and he will continue to ask me to dinner every Sunday or Monday.'

8 June: Theo and Jo come to see him, bringing the baby to whom he gives a bird's nest. *Marguerite Gachet at the Piano*. 'I am working much and fast, in that way I try to express the desperately rapid passing of things in modern life.'

6 July: Visits Theo in Paris. Learns that they plan to return to Holland. Lunch with Lautrec, sees Aurier; returns to Auvers disturbed.

7–12 July: *Wheatfield under Threatening Skies*.

16–23 July: *Ears of Wheat*. Seventy paintings and thirty drawings completed between 20 May and 27 July.

27 July: Shoots himself in the chest. Returns to the Café and goes up to his room.

28 July: Theo summoned to Auvers.

29 July: 1.30 am Dies, aged 37. 'I want to be going.' A letter to Theo found in his pocket. 'Well, the truth is, we can only make our pictures speak.'

30 July: Funeral, attended by Theo, Dr Gachet, Ravoux (owner of the café), Père Tanguy, Emile Bernard.

1891

25 January: Theo Van Gogh dies, in Utrecht, aged 34.

Window of Vincent's Studio in the Asylum in St Rémy, October 1889.

THE PLATES

Peasant Burning Weeds, 1883

30.5 × 39.5 cm. State Museum Kröller-Müller, Otterlo

The potato fields of Drenthe on a dour autumn day.

Van Gogh left The Hague in September 1883, having failed to achieve any sort of lasting domesticity with Sien. She had reverted to prostitution.

'How much sadness there is in life, but one must not, after all, grow melancholy and must look elsewhere, and working is the right thing.'

He drew dark, low-lying farmhouses awaiting winter, a barge being loaded with peat, a man dragging a harrow through heavy soil in preparation for sowing. ('I am ploughing on my canvas as they do on their fields.')

Desperate for companionship, and for someone to follow his example, he urged his brother Theo to give up art-dealing and become a painter himself. That, of course, would have meant destitution for them both. He eventually conceded that this would be so but protested 'I would not want to bloom if that meant you had to shrivel; I would not want to develop the artist in me if you had to repress the artist in you for my sake'.

Patting the small bonfire with his spade, the peasant clearing the ground momentarily becomes a devotee, tending the flame.

The Potato Eaters, 1885

82 × 114 cm. National Museum Vincent Van Gogh, Amsterdam

'I have tried to emphasize that those people eating their potatoes in the lamplight have dug the earth with those very hands they put into the dish and so it speaks of *manual labour* and how they have honestly earned their food.'

The pastor's son discovers, in a humble meal, vestiges of the Last Supper. The clock ticks beside the Crucifixion on the wall, the dish is shared, the cups are filled and passed round, the lamp burns. The De Groots are a Holy Family.

Van Gogh spent much of the winter of 1885 considering and rehearsing this his largest composition, making studies of hands outstretched to give and receive and of the four principal figures, gnarled yet bright-eyed. 'It might very well seem to be a *genuine peasant* painting,' he declared. He was insistent on this: 'When I call myself a peasant painter, it's a real fact.' Combining the emphatic qualities of the style of illustration he so admired in periodicals like *The Graphic* with the robust characteristics of Dutch low-life genre he put together a scene in which all is resolved. They are what they eat, so to speak. 'The colour they are painted in now is like the colour of a very dusty potato, unpeeled of course.' There's a rootedness, a sense of family security glimpsed through a window, an air of sufficiency and contentment that he both identified with and envied.

Peasant Cemetery, 1885

63 × 79 cm. National Museum Vincent Van Gogh, Amsterdam

On 26 March 1885 Pastor Theodorus Van Gogh of the Dutch Reformed Church in Nuenen died of a heart attack on his own doorstep. 'The first impact wasn't so much the shock of it as its gravity', Vincent wrote to Theo. 'Life is not long for anyone and the only thing that matters is what you do with it.'

The old church tower at Nuenen was a landmark, regarded by Van Gogh as the fixed point on the local horizon, whether glimpsed through the window of a weaver's cottage or seen all alone, in summer guarding the harvest fields, in winter capped with snow. For forty years it had been awaiting demolition.

In May 1885 the spire was removed. Van Gogh drew the crowd of busybodies at an informal auction of slates and other lumber, including the great iron cross. Much the same crowd as attended Courbet's *Burial at Ornans*, this time picking over the remains of the Catholic church itself.

Van Gogh decided to call his painting of the scene once the crowd had dispersed not *The Old Tower*, say, but *Peasant Cemetery*. 'That ruin tells me how a faith and a religion have mouldered away – strongly founded though they were – and how the life and death of peasant-folk remains forever the same, budding and withering like the grass and the flowers growing there.'

Weeds on the buttresses, belfry shutters askew, crows circling, door gaping: the stronghold of former certainties (Father Church, so to speak) stands derelict. The tower was finally pulled down in 1888.

'I wanted to express what a simple thing death and burial is, as simple as the falling of an autumn leaf – just a bit of earth turned over – a little wooden cross.'

Still Life with Open Bible, Candlestick and Novel, 1885

63 × 78 cm. National Museum Vincent Van Gogh, Amsterdam

The Family Bible lies open at the Book of Isaiah. Illegibly so, but the double-column brushwork is worthy of Frans Hals, whose example encouraged Van Gogh in the belief that black was not to be despised by true colourists. Hals, he reckoned, achieved at least twenty-seven varieties of black.

In this still life, put together six months after his father's death and painted 'in a rush, in one day', the blackness is fuggy, suggesting an all-night vigil before the candle was snuffed out. The Bible on its reading stand speaks the language the pastor best understood. Isaiah, chapter 53, verse 3: 'He is despised and rejected of men: a man of sorrows and acquainted with grief.' The thumbed yellow-back novel – Zola's relentlessly pessimistic *La Joie de Vivre* – is Vincent's rejoinder: Isaiah for modern times.

A strained if not barren relationship is here confessed. The father had been exasperated and distressed by the son's extreme behaviour, slumming among the miners of the Borinage, identifying with the poorest, living with a prostitute, outraging parishioners, refusing to eat properly.

What could Vincent say? 'One starts with a hopeless struggle to follow nature, and everything goes wrong; one ends by calmly creating from one's palette, and nature agrees with it and follows.'

In the autumn of 1885 his mother and youngest brother and sister prepared to leave the parsonage. Vincent himself, with lodgings elsewhere in Nuenen, was penniless. He collected birds' nests, keeping dozens in a cupboard. 'I shall do some drawings on the theme of nests and the birds in their nests inhabited by man, the huts on the heath and their inhabitants,' he told Theo. The severity of *Still Life with Open Bible* (the rectangular pages, the sharp white margins) contrasts with the humble nests, each so homely, each held in a confusion of twigs, each firmly lodged in a broken branch.

Le Moulin de Blute-Fin, Montmartre, 1886

45.4 × 37.5 cm. Glasgow Art Gallery and Museum

'There is – I believe – a school of impressionists. But I don't know much about them' (Letter to Theo, April 1885).

In 1885 Van Gogh's allegiance was still to 'Delacroix, Millet, Corot and the rest'. A year later his outlook shifted. Having spent three months in Antwerp, dedicated to life-study, admiring Rubens, diverted by Japanese prints, he moved to Paris in March 1886. Impressionism slowly affected him. There was a relaxation of symbolic intent, a lightening of the palette, a growing awareness of what could be achieved without impasto.

Living in Montmartre with Theo, he took to painting 'the huts on the heath and their inhabitants': the suburban perimeter with windmills on the skyline, quarries and fortifications below and beyond, a shanty area where a peasant way of life held out against urban and industrial development.

Le Moulin de Blute-Fin, Montmartre, painted towards the end of 1886, is more Corot than Pissarro. There is, as yet, no evidence of his 'trying to render intense colour and not a grey harmony'. The tricolour flies on the windmill and Van Gogh is doubtless reminded of the carpenter's yard seen from his window in The Hague as he fills in the details of each allotment.

A Basket of Bulbs, 1887

31.5 × 48 cm. National Museum Vincent Van Gogh, Amsterdam

'I have an idea for a kind of signboard, which I hope to carry out', Van Gogh wrote in February 1886. 'I mean, for instance, for a fishmonger, still life of fish, for flowers, for vegetables.' The idea was to promote the still life – indoors painting – to a more public domain.

A year later, living with Theo at 54 rue Lepic, Van Gogh painted a number of still lives of items close to hand: a clutch of novels, a pot of chives, herrings, a carafe and lemons and, twice, over, this basket of sprouting bulbs. Contained within the oval, snug as fledglings in a nest, they give promise of Impressionist stirrings in technique while anticipating spring.

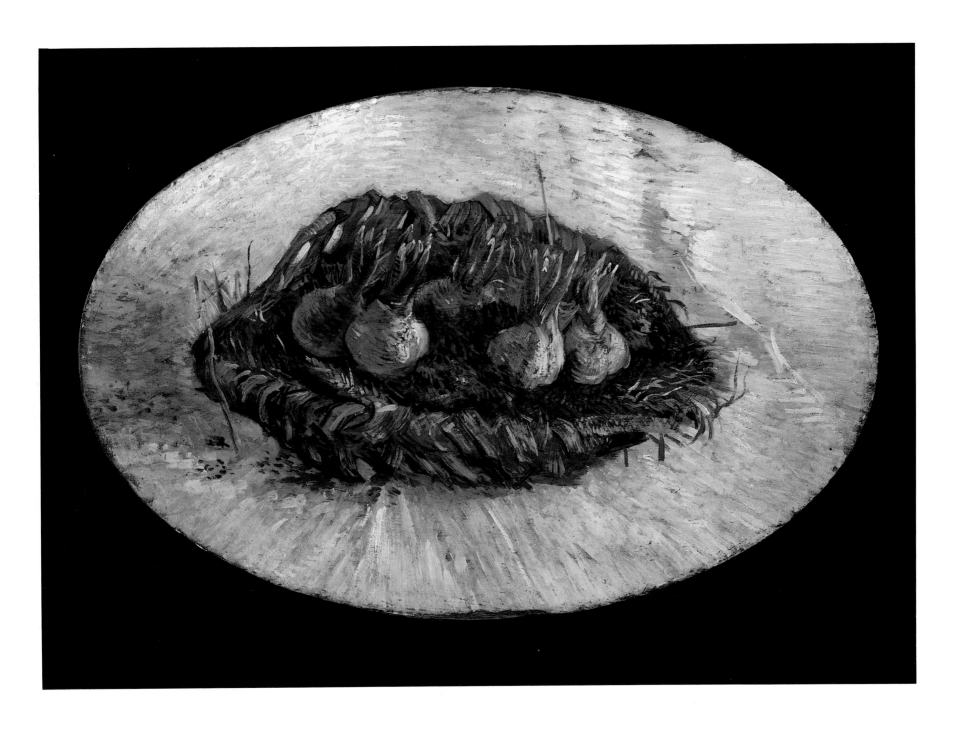

A Pair of Shoes, 1887

34 × 41.5 cm. Baltimore Museum of Art

Van Gogh painted shoes in 1887 because they were there: up to three pairs at a time. Like Sherlock Holmes (whose first published case, 'A Study in Scarlet' appeared in *Beeton's Christmas Annual* for 1887), Van Gogh read character from footwear. The boot unlaced, its tongue lolling here abuts its companion, upside down with the hobnails glinting.

The motif bears some relation to Theo and Vincent but it is, primarily, a representation of Vincent himself. 'An awkward customer', as a neighbour in one of the apartments as 54 rue Lepic remembered him. Van Gogh believed in walking; he had walked from Ramsgate to Welwyn via London to see his sister; he had tramped the roads of Drenthe; he regarded himself as a pilgrim painter, roughshod and undeviating. There may also be the implication that, as one shoe is useless without the other so too are he and Theo inseparable.

Skull, 1887/8

41.5 × 31.5 cm. National Museum Vincent Van Gogh, Amsterdam

Part of Van Gogh's intention, on moving to Paris, had been to study at life-drawing classes and to draw from the antique, that is, from plaster casts. The skull was part of the repertoire. In Antwerp he had painted a skeleton, on one occasion with a lit cigarette stuck between its teeth. Here, in one of two studies, the skull is presented as a *contre-jour* death's head.

Like his nests, his bulbs in a basket and, indeed, any one of his self-portraits, this skull serves as a sign. 'They persist nowadays in believing that *life is flat* and runs from birth to death', he wrote to Emile Bernard in June 1888. 'However life is probably round . . . ' The skull, the traditional *memento mori* used by artists down the ages to show the sitter's awareness that portraiture is vanity, grits its teeth and stares blankly.

After leaving Antwerp the twenty-five judges of student work there agreed that Van Gogh's work was so crude and inept it qualified only for the 8–10 year old class. The skull may be regarded as a challenge: Van Gogh's sign, exercise-book size, that he now knew the virtue of directitude. Placed in the category of (innocent) beginner he found himself capable of staring back at the life class. Pears, bulbs, potatoes, boots, books, skulls: he now had the formal ability to treat them as one.

Self-Portrait with Straw Hat, 1887

41 × 33 cm. National Museum Vincent Van Gogh, Amsterdam

Painted in the late summer of 1887 in his newly assimilated Impressionist style, thoroughly up-to-date with its sketchiness worthy of Toulouse-Lautrec (who was instrumental in getting him to move South the following year) and its tentative pointillism. The touches of red around the eyes and streaking from the mouth into the beard came from Van Gogh's study of Rubens. The hat, a colour essay in itself, fits him like a halo.

'It is a pity that as one gradually gains experience, one gradually loses one's youth.'

Portrait of Père Tanguy, 1887/8

92 × 75 cm. Musée Rodin, Paris

Van Gogh had already painted the dealer and colourman Père Tanguy a year before. Now, not long before he left Paris, he painted him again twice. This version, bought by Rodin from Tanguy's daughter, was painted as a form of payment. But it is an affectionate homage to 'si drôle de bon-homme' – 'such a funny fellow' – with every part of the picture animated in the latest styles: pointillism, of sorts, for the trousers, blues on blue for the jacket, and a background of transcribed Japanese prints.

With his flattened straw hat and narrowed eyes Père Tanguy is become somewhat Japanese himself. He merges with the ground where Mount Fuji, cherry blossom, snows and geisha, irises, streams and flowered meadows serve as Van Gogh's travel brochure. Somewhere, well away from Paris where, he declared to Gauguin, he found himself 'very miserable, quite ill, and almost addicted to drink', was a land where a painter could flourish.

'If I can live long enough', he wrote from Arles six months or so later, 'I shall be something like old Tanguy.' When he left Paris, Emile Bernard recalled, he covered the walls of the room he had painted in with Japanese prints. He told Bernard that this was to reassure Theo (who had become distracted by his garrulous, obsessive behaviour). As in the portraits of Père Tanguy, the walls were covered 'in such a way that my brother will think I am still here'.

Blossoming Almond in a Glass 1888

24 × 19 cm. National Museum Vincent Van Gogh, Amsterdam

Arriving in Arles on 20 February 1888, Van Gogh found deep snow ('really like the winter landscapes of the Japanese') turning to slush and a complete lack of the colourfulness he had expected. He felt stranded. 'The Museum's atrocious: an absolute joke.' There was a lack of people or things to reassure him. His first paintings, a landscape or two and still lives (clogs, potatoes), were little more than exercises to help get him accustomed.

Two small studies of a blossoming almond twig were a sign though of an unfolding to come. One, with a book placed on the table behind it, he sent to his sister Wil. The other, being uncluttered, was his frontispiece painting for Arles. Like a Manet flower study, it is a painting without complications. It has the simplicity Van Gogh associated with Japanese culture. It is a sudden display of virtuosity.

The blue streaks of shadow on yellow ground, the vermilion line on the wall, the green and brown twists of the branch and the fatty outbursts of the buds show what was to become the great characteristic of his art: Van Gogh's unerring touch when mood, circumstances, idea and available paint spontaneously combined.

Field with Flowers, 1888

54 × 65 cm. National Museum Vincent Van Gogh, Amsterdam

'A meadow full of very yellow buttercups, a ditch with irises, green leaves and purple flowers, the town in the background, some grey willows and a strip of blue sky.'

In his letters to Theo, in the sketches he scribbled between lines, and the drawings done as often after as before the main painting, Van Gogh staked his position. Each view that he discovered, as spring advanced, became a relevation. There was the sudden abundance of challenges to 'grey harmony', a rival to the old church tower of Nuenen. Orange pantiles instead of slates or thatch, 'that sea of gold with a band of purple irises': the language grew more exultant as his technique sprang into rapid service, the sky laid on thickly so as to counterbalance the serried meadow, the irises snapping open.

'Not a single flower is drawn completely so that they are mere dabs of colour, red, yellow, orange, green, blue, violet, but the impression of all these colours in their juxtaposition is there all right, in the painting as in nature.'

Van Gogh's admiration for John Constable, for a landscape art, Dutch bred, that gave equal weight to ditch and vista, is hinted at in this painting. The willows grow where once he would have put peasants. Now 'in the painting as in nature', there is no need to follow Millet too closely. Symbolic intent has no place in 'a Provençal orchard of *outstanding gaiety*'.

Harvest Landscape, 1888

72.5 × 92 cm. National Museum Vincent Van Gogh, Amsterdam

'I have a new subject in hand, fields green and yellow as far as the eye can see . . . It is exactly like a Solomon Konink, you know.'

He meant Philips de Koninck (1619–88), whose speciality was flat land, pale sea and vast clouded skies put together as much from the imagination as from topography. The Crau, 5 km outside Arles, painted in June as harvesting began, is a busy landscape. Montmajour sits on the far side, in strategic control of the plain, overlooking the railway that Van Gogh was to draw a month later. The farms are positioned like blockhouses, each surrounded by many yellows.

The wheel of the blue cart is the hub of the cycle of seasons. Under a sky so cloudless that it looks unchangeable, Van Gogh has established a complex account of reaping, carting, stacking and storing: the wide view from a vantage point beside an old mill.

Haystacks Near a Farm 1888

73 × 92.5 cm. State Museum Kröller-Müller, Otterlo

Placing himself by a pair of iron gates (that appear in other paintings of this farm) Van Gogh must have suddenly seen, in these upside down nests, the makings of an outsize still life. The stacks crowned with cohesive thatch, with ladders leaning against them like crutches, are unstable in a farmyard dotted and streaked with weeds. The woman with a pail leans towards them, adding to the impression of a task finished in haste.

Enclosing a drawing in a letter to Theo, Van Gogh wrote: 'The one with the stacks in the farmyard will appear too eccentric to you, but it was done in a great hurry, by way of a draft for a painting.' The painting has a masterly impatience – hardly any time to establish the trees or add chickens to the stubble. In his haste Van Gogh surpassed himself. 'I must warn you that everyone will think that I work too fast. Don't you believe a word of it.'

Sower with Setting Sun, 1888

64 × 80.5 cm. State Museum Kröller-Müller, Otterlo

'I imagine the man I have to paint, terrible in the furnace of the heat of harvest-time, as surrounded by the whole Midi.'

Seedtime and harvest, beginning and end, are combined in an image of transcendent energy. Drawings setting out Van Gogh's ideas for the painting suggest that the sower is walking a sea such as he had recently seen and drawn at Les Saintes-Maries-de-la-Mer. The stubble is burnished, the sun flowers rather than setting and the standing corn choruses and watches as the crows peck at the fallen seed.

'More and more it seems to me that the pictures which must be made so that painting should be wholly itself, and should raise itself to a height equivalent to the serene summits which the Greek sculptors or the German musicians, the writers of French novels reached, are beyond the power of an isolated individual: so they will probably be created by groups of men combining to execute an idea held in common.'

Van Gogh repeatedly voiced his hopes for a co-operative sort of art. He had suggested to Theo that he should join him as a painter, he had hopes of working in collaboration or commune with anyone who would agree: Gauguin, perhaps Emile Bernard, even perhaps Toulouse-Lautrec. In *The Sower* he takes a Millet and transforms it; he reaps Impressionism, harvests pointillism, advances his concept of the artist as provider, striding along with the sun at his shoulder. Such composite inspiration was, he felt, somewhat Japanese. 'One's sight changes; you see things with an eye more Japanese. You feel colours differently. The Japanese draw quickly, very quickly, like a lightning flash, because their nerves are finer, their feeling simpler.'

To be Japanese, Van Gogh was assuming, was to be like himself. The seasons merge, dawn and sunset, orient and occident, and, convinced that all arts combine, he wrote in June 1888 'I am reading a book on Wagner. What an Artist. One like that in painting would be something. *It will come.*'

Mousme Sitting in a Cane Chair, Half-Figure, 1888

74 × 60 cm. National Gallery of Art, Washington.

'A mousme is a Japanese girl – Provençal in this case – 12 to 14 years old.'

Van Gogh was preoccupied with the painting for a week in July 1888. Apart from an off-duty Zouave, the girl was his first sitter for months. He gave her oleander to hold. 'The oleander – Ah! that speaks of love and is beautiful like the Lesbos of Puvis de Chavannes, with women on the seashore.' Alert but modest she sits, not an intimate and no threat: a Provençale unaware that she is being made to substitute for some imagined Oriental.

Joseph Roulin, Sitting in a Cane Chair, Three-Quarter Length, 1888

81 × 65 cm. Museum of Fine Art, Boston

'Lets talk about Frans Hals', Van Gogh wrote to Emile Bernard at the time he painted Joseph Roulin, the Arles postal official, for the first time. 'Hammer into your head that master Frans Hals, that painter of all kinds of portraits, of a whole, gallant, live immortal republic.'

Roulin, seated in the same chair as the mousme, became a vital source of support for Van Gogh a few months later. 'A head somewhat like Socrates, hardly any nose at all, a high forehead, bald crown, little grey eyes, bright red chubby cheeks, a big pepper-and-salt beard, large ears. This man is an ardent republican and socialist, reasons quite well and knows a lot of things.'

Truculent, still astonished perhaps at being asked to pose ('the good fellow, unwilling as he was to accept money, *cost me more* in food and drink') is a Hals figure in modern dress. There's no Hals finesse in the clumsy uniform, the quick scrawl of frogging on the sleeves. 'To paint in one rush, as much as possible in one rush. What a joy to see such a Frans Hals . . . ' 'I use colour in a more arbitrary way to express myself forcefully.' Joseph Roulin has an expansive complexion, a beard that leaps off the face. His buttons are dabs, his fingers have a life of their own. 'What impassions me most' Van Gogh wrote to his sister Wilhelmien, 'is the portrait, the modern portrait.'

The Night Café, 1888

70 × 89 cm. Yale University Art Gallery

'In my picture of the "Night Café" I have tried to express the idea that the café is a place where one can ruin oneself, go mad or commit a crime.'

The Café de l'Alcazar, where Van Gogh lodged from April to September 1888 while aiming to move into the Yellow House, is represented as a waiting room for the shiftless, the ante-chamber to despair.

'It is the equivalent, though different, of the Potato Eaters.' Where the De Groots had been cosily lumped together, like birds in a nest, here solitary men are slumped. At a corner table a whore sits over a drink with her pimp. The chairs pushed back denote those who had homes to go to.

'To the great joy of the landlord, of the postman whom I had already painted, of the visiting night prowlers and of myself, for three nights running I sat up to paint and went to bed during the day.'

The joy has been painted out. Buzzing with sleeplessness the lamps halate, the yellow floorboards raked with sulphur seem barely contained by the stifling red and green of the walls. The billiard table stands like a bier in front of the bottle altar beneath the midnight clock.

'The picture is one of the ugliest I have done.'

Fourteen Sunflowers in a Vase, 1888

93 × 73 cm. National Gallery, London

Having rented the Yellow House in May, Van Gogh waited all summer before moving in: he hadn't the money to make it habitable until he received a small legacy from an uncle, enough to buy some chairs and other furniture. In August, anticipating Gauguin's arrival to share the house, he painted his first *Sunflowers*.

'Yellow is the embodiment of the utmost clarity of Love.' He intended a symphonic effect. 'Raw or broken chrome yellows will blaze forth on various backgrounds.' The sunflowers would furnish the small rooms, and they would produce 'the same kind of effect as Gothic church windows'.

With a rapidity worthy of Frans Hals, with a succulence, when still freshly painted, that must have made them glare on the pale blue walls, the sunflowers were a decorative scheme that represented Van Gogh's idea of 'an association of painters'. They were supposed to cast a benign glow over the work he and Gauguin would undertake. As he admitted a year later, 'to attain the high yellow note that I attained last summer I really had to be pretty well keyed up'.

Lieutenant Milliet, 1888

60 × 49 cm. State Museum Kröller-Müller, Otterlo

'I want to paint men and women with something of the eternal which the halo used to symbolize', Van Gogh wrote in August 1888. The following month he painted Second Lieutenant Milliet of the Zouaves, himself an amateur painter who went sketching with him to Montmajour. Years later Milliet recalled 'he painted too big, he didn't pay any attention to details, he didn't draw, you know'. He found Van Gogh 'very nervous'.

'The red kepi against an emerald-green background': instead of the halo there was the regimental insignia of moon and stars. Lieutenant Milliet wears a medal awarded for military service in Tonkin: he had gone East and, however prosaic his outlook, he represented, to Van Gogh, a connection with the Exotic.

'A fine subject.'

Les Alyscamps, 1888

73 × 92 cm. State Museum Kröller-Müller, Otterlo

Gauguin arrived in Arles on 23 October. The Alyscamps ('Elysian Fields'), the Roman cemetery in the town became a subject for both of them, a test of compatibility.

Gauguin treated the poplars and sarcophagi, ranged along an avenue, like anywhere else, outlining masses and filling them in thinly, exaggerating the autumn colours with his Symbolist palette. Van Gogh, encouraged by Gauguin to think badly of his whole approach, his 'rash and clumsy execution', created two banal and two dramatically formalized Alyscamps scenes.

'It is some poplar trunks cut by the frame where the leaves begin.' Between the trees the sarcophagi are lined up in perspective (outdoor versions of the billiard table in the Café de l'Alcazar) and the promenading figures are elongated in a Japanese manner.

Gauguin and Van Gogh went to Montpellier together and saw Courbet's *Bonjour, Monsieur Courbet* in the museum there. They also went on what Gauguin described as 'nocturnal promenades for reasons of hygiene' to the Maison Tutelle and other brothels. 'With Gauguin blood and sex prevail over ambition', Van Gogh wrote soon after Gauguin's arrival. In the Alyscamps he proved himself the one who appreciated the long, historical perspective of the place. Gauguin, in Arles on sufferance, painted like a tourist.

Vincent's Chair, 1888

93 × 73.5 cm. National Gallery, London

The chair is the man. Van Gogh had long thought so. He had been impressed by Luke Fildes' drawing (published in the Christmas 1870 number of *The Graphic*) showing Dickens' study immediately after he died, the writer's paraphernalia neatly laid out on the desk, the chair pushed aside.

It was 'quite amusing' he remarked, to portray character through the chair. By December 1888 relations with Gauguin were strained. 'Our arguments are terribly electric, sometimes we come out of them with our heads as exhausted as a used electric battery.' In such circumstances they were at opposite poles: Van Gogh saw himself by daylight, a plain peasant chair planted firmly on the floor, onions in a box behind. Very open. 'I tried for an effect of light by means of direct colour.'

The pipe and tobacco pouch were Van Gogh's usual attributes, though in this instance ('quite amusing') it is possible that the double-meaning of '*blague*' or tobacco pouch has a bearing on it. '*Blague*' is slang for nonsense. Though never one to ridicule himself, here Van Gogh is representing himself, compared to Gauguin, as guileless and uncomplicated. The bluff one. 'In any case', he wrote 'I must beware of my nerves.'

Gauguin's Chair, 1888

90.5 × 72 cm. National Museum Vincent Van Gogh, Amsterdam

Curving in all directions, with grasping arms and aggressive legs, this is the chair of a vehement man, the chair assigned to him by Van Gogh.

It basks in artificial light, the candle flame flaring sideways, the lamp on the wall more symbolic than actual. The restless, sarcastic Gauguin, full of ideas, braces himself. He was considering leaving. 'Vincent and I simply cannot live together in peace because of incompatability of temper.'

'Gauguin gives me the courage to imagine things and certainly things from the imagination take on a more mysterious character', Van Gogh wrote at the beginning of December. Then, on 23 December he wrote to Theo: 'Gauguin is very powerful, strongly creative, but just because of that he must have peace. Will he find it anywhere if he does not find it here? I am waiting for him to make a decision with absolute serenity.'

Within hours Van Gogh mutilated himself by cutting off the lobe of his left ear. The *Forum Republican*, Journal of the Arrondissement of Arles, reported:

'Last Sunday at 11.30 pm, one Vincent Vaugogh [*sic*], painter, of Dutch origin, presented himself at the maison de tolerance No.1, asked for one Rachel and gave her . . . his ear saying "Look after this object carefully". Then he disappeared.'

Augustine Roulin (La Berceuse), 1888/9

92 × 73 cm. State Museum Kröller-Müller, Otterlo

Five times over – creating a lullaby for himself – Van Gogh painted the same reassuring portrait of the wife of Roulin, the jovial post-office official who helped him home after the incident at the brothel and gave him much support in the subsequent weeks.

Madame Roulin sits in what could be Gauguin's chair, watching over the unseen cradle. Roulin himself and Dr Felix Rey of the Arles hospital were also painted against the busy wallpaper but it was she to whom Van Gogh kept returning. He thought of the composition as the centrepiece of a triptych, sunflowers on either side.

Writing to Gauguin, in late January, Van Gogh said 'As an impressionist arrangement of colours I have never invented anything better. And I believe that if one put this picture, such as it is, in a fisherman's boat, even Icelandic fishermen, there would be those who would feel inside there the cradle-song.'

He had conceived *The Sunflowers* as radiant, like 'Gothic church windows'. *La Berceuse*, the image of motherhood, was to be the embodiment of loving reassurance, 'the reds going to pure oranges, rising more in the flesh colours as far as the chromes merging into pinks and combining with olive and malachite greens'. *La Berceuse* was, by the fifth time he painted it, Van Gogh's final riposte to Gauguin.

Still Life with Onions and Book, 1889

50 × 64 cm. State Museum Kröller-Müller, Otterlo

'I am going to begin by doing one or two still lives so as to get back into the habit of painting.' It was the first week of January. Van Gogh had left the hospital and returned to the Yellow House for a few weeks until, in February, a further crisis put him back in hospital.

On the table he laid out what he had. His attributes: onions and tobacco pipe. His candle, still burning and a spent match beside a 'kind' letter from Theo, whose announcement that he was intending to get married had probably helped precipitate the breakdown before Christmas. The *Manuel Annuaire de la Santé ou Médecine et Pharmacie Domestiques* by F.V. Raspail was a popular medical companion. Remedies recommended by Raspail included onions.

Though a convalescent painting, this still life is as complex as any Van Gogh created. He assembles his hopes and flanks them with the empty bottle and the open kettle. Where once he placed his father's Bible now he relies on his own resources, and word from his distant brother.

Self-Portrait with Bandaged Ear, December 1889

60 × 49 cm. Courtauld Institute, London

'During my illness I saw again every room in the house at Zundert, every path, every plant in the garden, the views of the fields outside, the neighbours, the graveyard, the church, our kitchen garden at the back – down to a magpie's nest in a tall acacia in the graveyard.'

The print on the wall of the Yellow House signals still a world of bold lines and strong colours, a world he resignedly turns his back on. 'I am too old and (especially if I have a papier-mâché ear put on) too jerry-built to go there.'

In pose he begins to resemble Père Tanguy, but it is the buttoned-up convalescent, allowed out because he has apparently made a good recovery, who stares so. 'Serenity returns to my brain day by day', he reassured Theo. But he also said 'If I did not have your friendship I should be remorslessly driven to suicide, and, cowardly as I am, I should commit it in the end.'

The Crau with Peach Trees in Bloom, 1889

65.5 × 81.5 cm. Courtauld Institute, London

Writing to the painter Paul Signac, who had visited him in hospital, Van Gogh described seeing and painting his second spring in the Crau.

'A poor landscape with little cottages, blue skyline of the Alpine foothills, sky white and blue. The foreground, patches of land surrounded by cane hedges, where small peach trees are in bloom – everything is small there, the gardens, the fields, the orchards, and the trees, even the mountains, as in certain Japanese landscapes, which is the reason why the subject attracted me.'

The view reminiscent of Philips de Koninck has shifted. The blue cart is now on the extreme left and peach trees flourish where previously, it seems, they had been edited out. Celebrating his days of release from hospital, Van Gogh aerates the sky with shimmering dots, reminiscent of Signac's pointillism, and flecks the whole picture with the goose-pimples raised by the cold, dry Mistral wind.

Soon after this Theo wrote to tell him he had married Johanna Bonger, on 17 April. Another crisis, as a result of which (and of the hostility whipped up in Arles against him) it was decided that Van Gogh should go to the 'Maison de Santé' at Saint-Rémy de Provence, near Tarascon.

Dormitory in the Hospital, 1889

74 × 92 cm. Private collection

Painted from memory, at Saint-Rémy. The perspective of *The Night Café* lengthens into another sort of dreariness. Draped beds with labels identifying each patient are substituted for the marble-topped tables, a crucifix hangs in place of the clock.

The hospital had been a refuge from pestering children egged on by hostile adults who got up a petition demanding Van Gogh's committal as a madman. The staff had been sympathetic. But there was no privacy, no long-term prospect. At Saint-Rémy, admitted as a third-class inmate 'to prevent a recurrence of previous attacks', he had at least a room of his own with another available as a studio.

'What you ought to know', Theo wrote, 'is that from one point of view you are not to be pitied, though it may not seem so.'

Mountain Landscape Seen across the Walls with Rising Sun and Green Field, 1889

72 × 92 cm. State Museum Kröller-Müller, Otterlo

Through the bars of his upstairs cell Van Gogh could see the Alpilles beyond the cloister garden wall. Omitting the bars he painted the enclosure again and again, showing the wheat growing, ripening, being reaped. He telescoped the hills into mountainous encroachments and set the walls tilting wildly.

The monk and the painter here coincide. 'I have been "in a hole" all my life, and my mental condition is not only vague *now*, but *has always been so*, so that whatever is done for me, I *cannot* think things out so as to balance my life.'

In the asylum, he wrote, 'you continually hear terrible cries and howls like beasts in a menagerie'. He was allowed out, with an escort, into the grounds and the neighbourhood. 'When I am working in the garden they all come to look, and I assure you they have the discretion and manners to leave me alone – more than the good people of the town of Arles, for instance.'

The wall rides the field, flinging itself across, warding off the world beyond where the sun looms more orientally than ever.

Wheat Field with Cypresses, 1889

72 × 91 cm. National Gallery, London

Though the cypresses respond to the agitated sky, the bushes squirm and the wheat ripples, this study of a corner of a field just beyond the cloister walls is a landscape of mood comparable to *Chill October* by the former Pre-Raphaelite John Millais, which he had seen in 1875.

'I have always remembered some English pictures such as "Chill October",' he wrote in 1884. Where Millais concentrated on the grey harmony of autumn coming on, sedge withering and trees dimming as evening draws in, Van Gogh put all his energy into the convulsions of high summer with a Mistral blowing: the landscape of the South distantly echoing that of the reticent North.

Starry Night, 1889

73 × 92 cm. Museum of Modern Art, New York

'The cypresses are always occupying my thoughts. I should like to make something of them like the canvases of the sunflowers because it astonishes me that they have *not yet been done as I* see them.'

Furious, italicized, the trees join forces with the rampaging night sky. Winds suffused with brimming stars, adorned with Lieutenant Milliet's moon insignia, storm the land.

'Why, I ask myself, shouldn't the shining dots of the sky be as accessible as the black dots on the map of France? Just as we take a train to reach Tarascon or Rouen, we take death to reach a star.'

That summer at Saint-Rémy Van Gogh had been reading Shakespeare. Hence, perhaps, 'the floor of heaven . . . thick inlaid with patines of bright gold'. By late June (when he painted *Starry Night*) he was half way, he said, through *Henry V*, reaching the finest rhetoric.

'And those that leave their valiant bones in France,
Dying like men, though buried in your dung-hills,
They shall be fam'd; for there the sun shall greet them,
And draw their honours reeking up to heaven'.

The bars of the cell have fallen away. The cypresses aspire. 'Under the great starlit vault of heaven something which after all one can only call God.'

Self-Portrait, 1889

65 × 54 cm. Musée d'Orsay, Paris

'This new attack, old chap, seized me on a windy day in the fields when I was in the midst of painting. I finished the canvas nevertheless. I will send it to you.'

Periods of particular lucidity often precede epileptic attacks, and what was true of Dostoievsky appears to have been true of Van Gogh. Painting 'day in day out', as he said, 'to avoid being distracted' he drove himself to collapse. The pallor of this self-portrait partly stems from his lack of colours: Prussian blue, chrome yellow and white were his main resort. But there is an intensity stemming from extreme, rapid concentration. 'Work . . . will be the best lightning conductor for my malady.' Not knowing the reason for his afflication (syphilis acquired in Antwerp, perhaps, manic-depressive behaviour brought on by circumstances, some form of epilepsy or inherited instability), Van Gogh could only attempt to live through it to some purpose.

The greenish flames belong to the iconography of passion, but for Van Gogh they are more immediate: wallpaper grown vibrant, mood turned horrific, something of what he had perceived in the atmosphere of *The Night Café*: 'an atmosphere like a devil's furnace, of pale sulphur'.

Pieta (after Delacroix), 1889

73 × 60.5 cm. National Museum Vincent Van Gogh, Amsterdam

In July Jo, his sister-in-law, wrote saying she was pregnant and asking him to be godfather. The news disturbed him. He went to Arles to collect some paintings, saw Rachel the prostitute and returned to Saint-Rémy delirious. 'For many days together I have been *absolutely* distraught as at Arles, quite as badly, if not worse.'

'During my illness a misfortune happened to me – that lithograph of Delacroix, the 'Pieta', fell with some other prints into some oil and paint and was ruined. I was upset about it – so I made myself sit down and paint it.'

Copying was a means of reinvigorating himself. Emboldened in the transcription, suffused once again with colour, Van Gogh's Delacroix is a Delacroix reanimated. 'I hope it has feeling', he wrote.

'My mind clear and my fingers so sure of themselves.' Though confined, and seeing other art in print form only, Van Gogh found himself retracing what he admired: it was a return to his original passions, the honesty of Millet, the vitality of Delacroix. Copying was both exercise and homage. It also represented Van Gogh's striving for a common language in which all would be reconciled, like to like, 'marrying form and colour'.

The Artist's Bedroom in Arles, 1889

56.5 × 74 cm. Musée d'Orsay, Paris

The first version of *The Artist's Bedroom* was painted in October 1888, soon after Van Gogh moved into the Yellow House.

'I wanted to achieve an effect of simplicity of the sort one finds in "Felix Holt". After being told this you may quickly understand the picture.'

George Eliot's *Felix Holt* ends with contentment as Esther resolves to marry the good Felix. For this scene 'Esther chose to sit in the kitchen, in the wicker chair against the white table, between the fire and the window. The kettle was singing and the clock was ticking steadily towards four o'clock.' All's well and security for life is achieved.

In Van Gogh's bedroom 'colour is to do everything', he wrote, and 'giving by its simplification a grander style to things, is to be suggestive here of *rest* and sleep in general'.

The two versions done in the autumn of 1889, at Saint-Rémy, have the same essentials: the sturdy bed, the wash-stand, the two chairs. The paintings on the walls alter, but the snugness remains. The room has been opened out like a stage set. Here, demonstrably, lies contentment. His cell at Saint-Rémy had green curtains with roses on, 'relics of some rich and ruined deceased'. Painting 'duplicates for family and friends' of a composition in which he itemized furniture he actually owned, in a house he had regarded as his, was 'comfortable, as music is comforting', he said. 'It does me good and drives away, I think, the abnormal ideas.'

The Ravine, 1889

73 × 92 cm. State Museum Kröller-Müller, Otterlo

The stream runs through cavities in the limestone of the Alpilles at 'Les Peyroulets' ('little saucepans'), a gorge some distance from Saint-Rémy. Van Gogh went there with a warder who knew the area.

This is the second version of the landscape, painted in December 1889. Of the ten paintings Van Gogh showed the following March at the Société des Artistes Indépendents, *The Ravine* was the one that brought most comment. While Theo told him that Pissarro had mentioned that 'Monet said that your pictures were the best of all in the exhibition', Gauguin wrote saying 'to many artists you are the most remarkable one in the exhibition' and went on to suggest a swap. 'I should like to exchange with you for anything of mine you choose. The one I mean is a mountainous landscape: two very small travellers seem to be climbing in search of the unknown. It's beautiful and impressive. I've talked at length about it with Aurier, Bernard and many others. All congratulate you.'

Les Ravines had its impact on the School of Pont-Aven. In Van Gogh's œuvre it marks the onset of a particularly turbulent phase. The clumps of scrub flame on the slopes and the stream 'white and foaming like soap-suds', he wrote to his mother, force the pace.

During December, over Christmas, he suffered two attacks and a relapse.

Noon: Rest (after Millet), 1890

73 × 92 cm. Musée d'Orsay, Paris

Kept indoors by bad weather and his nervous state, Van Gogh painted a number of copies after Daumier, Doré and, particularly, Millet in December–January 1889–90. He worked from engravings, 'translating into another language, the language of colours'.

Noon is Millet, 'the voice of the wheat' rendered cloudless and golden. Van Gogh repays previous borrowings: the tousled straw, the pair of shoes and the pair of sickles resting together. From Millet Van Gogh had derived his peasantry language, the concentration on moments when labour appears dignified, wholly responsible, diurnal.

This image *Les Sommelliers*, shows blissful peace after productive hours. The painting preaches basic contentment.

'The *interpretation* of the composer is something, and it is not a hard and fast rule that only the composer should play his own composition.'

Prisoners Round (after Doré), 1890

80 × 64 cm. Pushkin Museum, Moscow

Taken from one of Gustave Doré's illustrations, engraved by H. Pisan, for his huge volume *London*, 1872.

This is not just Newgate prison but also, clearly, the universal plight of the prisoner, whether convict or asylum inmate. Van Gogh had read an article on Dostoievsky's *Notes from the House of the Dead*: the exercise yard rehearses his thoughts.

'Many people do not copy, many others do – started on it accidentally and I find that it teaches me things, and above all it sometimes gives me consolation.'

The prison walls, coloured by Van Gogh, change from grey to yellow as they open to the light. Two butterflies flutter far above the prisoners' heads. Doré's London, which was also Van Gogh's London shortly after, was a place of melodramatic contrasts: high life in Richmond or Rotten Row and, over the page, dismal squalor down in the docks or beneath railway arches. The *Prisoners' Round* is the oppressive monotony of a built-up society. The vertical pit-shaft of despair contrasts with the sprawling ease of *Les Sommelliers*.

Branches of an Almond Tree in Blossom, 1890

73 × 92 cm. State Museum Vincent Van Gogh, Amsterdam

'Today I received your good news that you are at last a father, that the most critical time is over for Jo, and finally that the little boy is well.'

'We shall give him your name', Theo wrote. 'My wish is that he will have the same perseverance and will be just as courageous as you.' He enclosed an article that had appeared in the *Mercure de France*: 'Les Isolés, by Albert Aurier; the first full appreciation of Van Gogh to be published, a hectic one to say the least. ('In his categorical affirmation of the essential character of things, in his often rash simplication of form, in his insolent desire to look at the sun face to face, in the passion of his drawing and colour, there lies revealed a powerful one, a male, a darer . . .')

Van Gogh responded at length to Aurier. 'Many thanks for your article . . . which greatly surprised me. I like it very much as a work of art in itself, in my opinion your words are colourful, in short, I rediscover my canvases in your article, but better than they are, richer, more full of meaning.'

Meanwhile he began a painting celebrating the birth. 'I started straight away making a picture for him, to hang in their bedroom, big branches of white almond blossom against a blue sky,' he told his mother.

This was a painting to be gazed up into, a painting to herald growth and renewal. He probably used cut branches but, unlike the almond twig in a glass, painted in Arles two years before, here the branches take over, crowding in from three sides in family celebration.

In August 1880 he had written to Theo 'you see that I am in a rage of work, though for the moment it doesn't produce very brilliant results. But I hope these thorns will bear their white blossoms in due time, and that this apparently sterile struggle is none other than the labour of childbirth. First pain, then the joy.'

In late February 1890, Van Gogh suffered a ten-month breakdown. 'My work was going well,' he wrote in April. 'the last canvas of branches in bloom – you will see that it was perhaps the best, the most patiently worked thing I had done, painted with calm and with a greater firmness of touch. And the next day, down like a brute.'

Vase with Violet Irises, 1890

92 × 73.5 cm. Metropolitan Museum, New York

On 16 May Dr Peyron noted: 'Today he requests his release to go and live in the north of France, in the hope that the climate will prove more favourable.'

The irises, bursting from the vase in reckless profusion, were part of Van Gogh's last minute attempt to embrace the South. 'I saw the country again, fresh and full of flowers after the rain – how many things there were I could still have made.'

Keyed up, anticipating the move, he painted furiously for a fortnight, from early morning until night. 'The brush strokes come like clockwork.' Where he had originally intended his sunflowers to be golden against royal blue, here contrast is reversed and the blooms are haloed.

On meeting him, for the first time, on 17 May in Paris, Jo Van Gogh-Bonger was surprised. 'I had expected a sick man, but here was a sturdy, broad-shouldered man, with a healthy colour, a smile on his face and a very resolute appearance.'

Road with Men Walking, 1890

92 × 73 cm. State Museum Kröller-Müller, Otterlo

Irises, roses, a field with butterflies, a version of Rembrandt's *Raising of Lazarus* and 'finally a "Cypress with a Star"'. The last paintings produced in Saint-Rémy were a resumé made urgent by expectation.

Road with Men Walking (Cypress with a Star) is *Starry Night* dying down, the night sky seething less, the cypress calmer, the ground streaming along in the same magnetic field.

'The north will interest me like a new country', Van Gogh wrote. 'My wish to leave here now is imperative.' In the painting, under 'a moon lacking radiance', a carriage approaches, overtaking 'two belated pedestrians. Very romantic maybe, but also Provence, I think.'

The Alpilles swing round from the left, the further cypresses, guarding the cottage, put up their protective, four-poster coverage, the road presses on. This is the end of the working day, the close of a period, for Van Gogh, of being far removed, communicating – if not by painting – by letter.

The Church in Auvers, 1890

94 × 74 cm. Musée d'Orsay, Paris

The same approach as *Road with Men Walking*, only here, in Auvers-sur-Oise not far from Paris, the path divides and the church stands bolder than any cypress.

'It is almost the same thing as the studies I made at Nuenen of the old tower and the churchyard, though now the colour is probably more expressive, more sumptuous.'

Back in the North Van Gogh encountered again the dominance of the village church, the lofty belfry, the shouldering aisle roof, the stout buttresses. High summer brings blue and green. 'The building appears purplish against a deep blue sky, of pure cobalt; the stained glass windows appear like blotches of ultramarine blue, the roof is purple and in part orange. In the foreground some green plants in bloom.'

Doctor Gachet, 1890

68 × 57 cm. Musée d'Orsay, Paris

Dr Paul-Ferdinand Gachet was a specialist in nervous diseases, a believer in homeopathic medicine and an amateur artist. He had lived in Auvers since 1872 and practised three days a week in Paris. Pissarro recommended him to Theo in October 1889: from then on the plan was to establish Vincent where Gachet could keep an eye on him.

The two men hit it off. Van Gogh discovered a pleasing melancholy in Gachet. 'He lost his wife some years ago, which greatly contributes to his being a broken man . . . he is as disorganized about his job as a doctor as I am about my painting.' Warming to him he declared him 'something like another brother, so much do we resemble each other physically and also mentally'.

'A sun-tanned face the colour of an overheated brick with red hair and a white cap.' Dr Gachet had a printing press and encouraged Van Gogh to make etchings. He had him to dinner every Sunday or Monday, showed him his Pissarro and his Cézannes. 'To use the expression "Love of Art" is hardly an exact term' he said. 'It is the word "Belief" that should be used, belief, just to the point of martyrdom.'

Van Gogh's sentiments exactly. Sitting for him, Gachet adopted the pose of sympathetic listener holding foxgloves denoting a natural remedy. This is the second version of the portrait. 'M. Gachet is absolutely *fanatical* about this portrait and wants me to do one for him.'

'I should like to paint portraits which would appear after a century to the people living then as apparitions. By which I mean that I do not endeavour to achieve this by photographic resemblance but by means of our impassioned expressions – that is to say, using our knowledge of and our modern taste for colour.'

Marguerite Gachet at the Piano, 1890

102 × 50 cm. Kunstmuseum Basel

In the last week of June Van Gogh painted this portrait, envisaging it hung next to a horizontal painting of a wheat field. 'We are still far from the time when people will understand the curious relation between one fragment of nature and another which all the same explain each other and enhance each other.'

Dr Gachet's daughter occupies the same size canvas as, for example, *Wheat Field under Threatening Skies*. She provides musical accompaniment. 'The dress is pink, the wall in the background green with orange dots, the carpet red with green dots, the piano dark violet.' The dots are orchestrated, pushing upwards, swirling through the skirt and peppering the wall.

'A figure I did with pleasure – but difficult.' Marguerite Gachet is absorbed in her pose at the keyboard, a disassociated figure, unlike Gachet who comes close, like a mirror image.

Landscape with Carriage and Train in the Distance, 1890

72 × 90 cm. Pushkin Museum, Moscow

'Some fields seen from a height with a road and a little carriage on it.'

Where the blue cart had stood in his paintings of the Crau, where a plough stands in Millet's painting *Winter, the plain of Chantilly* (copied by Van Gogh six months before) here the carriage heads one way, the train streaming clouds in the opposite direction. Van Gogh has positioned himself overlooking the fields of both his 'campaign in the South' and his affiliations in the North: Millet, Pissarro and, beyond them, Ruysdael and Philips de Koninck. The glistening wet road, the patches of crops, poppies and walls and tiled roofs put what he had learned around Arles into a fresh light.

Ears of Wheat, June 1890

64.5 × 47 cm. National Museum Vincent Van Gogh, Amsterdam

In mid-June Van Gogh wrote Gauguin a letter he never sent.

'Look, here's an idea may suit you. I am trying to do some studies of wheat like this (but I can't seem to draw it), nothing but ears of wheat with blue-green stalks, long leaves like ribbons of green shot with pink, ears that are just turning yellow, edged with the soft pink of the dusty bloom – a pink bindweed down below twisted round a stem.'

The field of vision entirely filled with growth and abundance. The wheat field at Saint-Rémy tilting up, the butterflies on grass painted just before he left Saint-Rémy, and the almond branches celebrating the birth of his nephew. *Ears of Wheat* ('the soft rustle of the ears as they sway in the breeze') is a culmination: Van Gogh at his most direct. The bird's nest, the bulbs, the haystack, the skull, the sunflowers, the head of Joseph Roulin with flowing beard: the wheat field combines them all. Closing in, cropping the image arbitrarily, ignoring distance, in effect eliminating perspective, turning the Japanese ideal and the background rhythms of wallpaper into a kind of chorus ('Millet . . . the voice of the wheat' amplified) Van Gogh achieves formal and emotional unison.

'What the germinating force is in the grain of the wheat, *love is in us*' (Paris, 1887).

'What else can one do, when we think of all the things we do not know the reason for, than go to look at a field of wheat? The history of those plants is like our own; for aren't we, who live on bread, to a considerable extent like wheat, at least aren't we forced to submit to growing like a plant without the power to move . . . ' (Saint-Rémy, 1889).

Wheat Field under Threatening Skies, 8/9 July 1890

50.5 × 100.5 cm. National Museum Vincent Van Gogh, Amsterdam

'They are vast stretches of cornfield under troubled skies, and I did not need to go out of my way to try to express sadness and the extreme of loneliness. I hope you will see them soon – for I hope to bring them to you in Paris as soon as possible since I almost think that these canvases will tell you, what I meant to say in words, the *health and strengthening* that I see in the country.'

This painting, so obviously disturbed, is too easily interpreted as Van Gogh's last: a painting in which paths stretch like arms and legs flung across the corn and crows rise, as though alarmed by a gun shot.

But it was painted more than a fortnight before Van Gogh borrowed a pistol from his landlord 'to shoot crows'. He had just returned from seeing Theo in Paris. 'Back here I still felt very sad and continued to feel the storm which threatens you weighing on me also. What was to be done – you see I try generally to be fairly cheerful, but my life too is threatened at the very root, and my steps too are wavering.'

In other paintings done at the same time, 'vast spaces of corn after the rains', everything conspires to suggest agoraphobia. The fields lose contact with the ground, the skies bustle incoherently and bunting hangs in front of the Town Hall of Auvers for an unattended Bastille Day. Roots and trees fight one another, a man on a roof struggles with the thatch.

Landscape in the Rain, July 1890

50 × 100 cm. National Museum of Wales

Auvers in rain, Auvers nestling, roofs tucked among the trees and only the church tower standing out against the hillside. The scene has all the makings of a failed harvest, after Hokusai.

'We do not feel we are dying, but we do feel the truth that we are of small account, and that we are paying a hard price to be a link in the chain of artists, in health, in youth, in liberty, none of which we enjoy' (letter to Theo, May 1888).

Van Gogh lived to see the harvest of 1890 begun, the reaped wheat bundled into stooks, the stubble ready for burning. While the rain lasted, though, he saw only the blurring, the dissolving, the sodden fields lying open like the illegible pages of the family bible.

'For he shall grow up . . . as a tender plant, and as a root out of a dry ground: he hath no form nor comeliness: and when we shall see him there is no beauty that we should desire him.

'He is despised and rejected of men: a man of sorrows and acquainted with grief . . . he was despised and we esteemed him not.

'Surely he hath borne our griefs, and carried our sorrows: yet we did esteem him stricken, smitten of God and afflicted.'

Isaiah Chapter 53 (see Plate 4)

At the graveside on the afternoon of 30 July 1890, a hot day, Dr Gachet spoke.

'He was an honest man and a great artist. He had only two aims, mankind and art.' Weeping, he offered his prognosis. 'Art he loved above everything, and it will make him live.'

LIST OF COLOUR PLATES

45: *Peasant Burning Weeds*, 1883, oil on panel, 30.5 × 39.5 cm. State Museum Kröller-Müller, Otterlo.

47: *The Potato Eaters*, 1885, oil on canvas, 82 × 114 cm. National Museum Vincent Van Gogh, Amsterdam.

49: *Peasant Cemetery*, 1885, oil on canvas, 63 × 79 cm. National Museum Vincent Van Gogh, Amsterdam.

51: *Still Life with Open Bible, Candlestick and Novel*, 1885, oil on canvas, 63 × 78 cm. National Museum Vincent Van Gogh, Amsterdam.

53: *Le Moulin de Blute-Fin, Montmartre*, 1886, oil on canvas, 45.4 × 37.5 cm. Glasgow Art Gallery and Museum.

55: *A Basket of Bulbs*, 1887, oil on panel, 31.5 × 48 cm. National Museum Vincent Van Gogh, Amsterdam.

57: *A Pair of Shoes*, 1887, oil on canvas, 34 × 41.5 cm. Baltimore Museum of Art.

59: *Skull*, 1887/8, oil on canvas, 41.5 × 31.5 cm. National Museum Vincent Van Gogh, Amsterdam.

61: *Self-Portrait with Straw Hat*, 1887, oil on cardboard, 41 × 33 cm. National Museum Vincent Van Gogh, Amsterdam.

63: *Portrait of Père Tanguy*, 1887/8, oil on canvas, 92 × 75 cm. Musée Rodin, Paris.

65: *Blossoming Almond in a Glass*, 1888, oil on canvas, 24 × 19 cm. National Museum Vincent Van Gogh, Amsterdam.

67: *Field with Flowers*, 1888, oil on canvas, 54 × 65 cm. National Museum Vincent Van Gogh, Amsterdam.

69: *Harvest Landscape*, 1888, oil on canvas, 72.5 × 92 cm. National Museum Vincent Van Gogh, Amsterdam.

71: *Haystacks Near a Farm*, 1888, oil on canvas, 73 × 92.5 cm. State Museum Kröller-Müller, Otterlo.

73: *Sower with Setting Sun*, 1888, oil on canvas, 64 × 80.5 cm. State Museum Kröller-Müller, Otterlo.

75: *Mousme Sitting in a Cane Chair, Half-Figure*, 1888, oil on canvas, 74 × 60 cm. National Gallery of Art, Washington.

77: *Joseph Roulin, Sitting in a Cane Chair, Three-Quarter Length*, 1888, oil on canvas, 81 × 65 cm. Museum of Fine Art, Boston.

79: *The Night Café*, 1888, oil on canvas, 70 × 89 cm. Yale University Art Gallery.

81: *Café Terrace at Night*, 1888, oil on canvas, 81 × 65.5 cm. State Museum Kröller-Müller, Otterlo.

83: *Fourteen Sunflowers in a Vase*, 1888, oil on canvas, 93 × 73 cm. National Gallery, London.

85: *Lieutenant Milliet*, 1888, oil on canvas, 60 × 49 cm. State Museum Kröller-Müller, Otterlo.

87: *Les Alyscamps*, 1888, oil on canvas, 73 × 92 cm. State Museum Kröller-Müller, Otterlo.

89: *Vincent's Chair*, 1888, oil on canvas, 93 × 73.5 cm. National Gallery, London.

91: *Gauguin's Chair*, 1888, oil on canvas, 90.5 × 72 cm. National Museum Vincent Van Gogh, Amsterdam.

93: *Augustine Roulin (La Berceuse)*, 1888/9, oil on canvas, 92 × 73 cm. State Museum Kröller-Müller, Otterlo.

95: *Still Life with Onions and Book*, 1889, oil on canvas, 50 × 64 cm. State Museum Kröller-Müller, Otterlo.

97: *Self-Portrait with Bandaged Ear*, December 1889, oil on canvas, 60 × 49 cm. Courtauld Institute, London.

99: *The Crau with Peach Trees in Bloom*, 1889, oil on canvas, 65.5 × 81.5 cm. Courtauld Institute, London.

101: *Dormitory in Hospital*, 1889, oil on canvas, 74 × 92 cm. Private collection.

103: *Mountain Landscape Seen across the Walls with Rising Sun and Green Field*, 1889, oil on canvas, 72 × 92 cm. State Museum Kröller-Müller, Otterlo.

105: *Wheat Field with Cypresses*, 1889, oil on canvas, 72 × 91 cm. National Gallery, London.

107: *Starry Night*, 1889, oil on canvas, 73 × 92 cm. Museum of Modern Art, New York.

109: *Self-Portrait*, 1889, oil on canvas, 65 × 54 cm. Musée d'Orsay, Paris.

111: *Pieta (after Delacroix)*, 1889, oil on canvas, 73 × 60.5 cm. National Museum Vincent Van Gogh, Amsterdam.

113: *The Artist's Bedroom in Arles*, 1889, oil on canvas, 56.5 × 74 cm. Musée d'Orsay, Paris.

115: *The Ravine*, 1889, oil on canvas, 73 × 92 cm. State Museum Kröller-Müller, Otterlo.

117: *Noon: Rest (after Millet)*, 1890, oil on canvas, 73 × 92 cm. Musée d'Orsay, Paris.

119: *Prisoners' Round (after Doré)*, 1890, oil on canvas, 80 × 64 cm. Pushkin Museum, Moscow.

121: *Branches of an Almond Tree in Blossom*, 1890, oil on canvas, 73 × 92 cm. National Museum Vincent Van Gogh, Amsterdam.

123: *Vase with Violet Irises*, 1890, oil on canvas, 92 × 73.5 cm. Metropolitan Museum, New York.

125: *Road with Men Walking*, 1890, oil on canvas, 92 × 73 cm. State Museum Kröller-Müller, Otterlo.

127: *The Church in Auvers*, 1890, oil on canvas, 94 × 74 cm. Musée d'Orsay, Paris.

129: *Doctor Gachet*, 1890, oil on canvas, 68 × 57 cm. Musée d'Orsay, Paris.

131: *Marguerite Gachet at the Piano*, 1890, oil on canvas, 102 × 50 cm. Kunstmuseum, Basel.

133: *Landscape with Carriage and Train in the Distance*, 1890, oil on canvas, 72 × 90 cm. Pushkin Museum, Moscow.

135: *Ears of Wheat*, June 1890, oil on canvas, 64.5 × 47 cm. National Museum Vincent Van Gogh, Amsterdam.

137: *Wheat Field under Threatening Skies*, July 1890, oil on canvas, 50.5 × 100.5 cm. National Museum Vincent Van Gogh, Amsterdam.

139: *Landscape in the Rain*, July 1890, oil on canvas, 50 × 100 cm. National Museum of Wales.

LIST OF BLACK AND WHITE PLATES

6: *Self-Portrait*, Oct/Dec 1887, oil, 47 × 35 cm. Musée d'Orsay, Paris.

7: *The Yellow House in Arles*, September 1888, chalk, pen, brown ink, watercolour, 25.5 × 31.5 cm. National Museum Vincent Van Gogh, Amsterdam.

8: *Sunflowers*, 1887, oil, 43 × 61 cm. Metropolitan Museum of Art, New York

9: *Dance Hall with Dancing Women*, November 1885, black and coloured chalk, 9 × 16 cm. National Museum Vincent Van Gogh, Amsterdam.

10: *Gas Tanks near the Hague*, 1882, chalk and pencil, 24 × 33.5 cm. National Museum Vincent Van Gogh, Amsterdam.

11: *Wheatfield with Sheaves and Windmill*, August 1885, black chalk, 22.5 × 29.5 cm. National Museum Vincent Van Gogh, Amsterdam.

13: *Carpenter's Yard and Laundry*, 1882, 28.5 × 47 cm. State Museum Kröller-Müller, Otterlo.

14: *The Chair*, 1890, pencil, 33 × 24.5 cm. National Museum Vincent Van Gogh, Amsterdam.

15: *The Potato Eaters*, 1885, lithograph, Stedelijk Museum, Amsterdam.

16–17: *Women Carrying Coal*, autumn 1882, watercolour, 32 × 50 cm. State Museum Kröller-Müller, Otterlo.

18: *Mlle Gachet in her Garden*, June 1890, 46 × 55 cm. Musée d'Orsay, Paris.

19: *Portrait of the Artist's Mother*, Oct 1888, oil, Christie's, London.

20: *Portrait of Dr Rey*, January 1889, oil, 64 × 53 cm. Hermitage Museum, Leningrad.

21: *Self-Portrait*, March 1887, oil, State Museum Kröller-Müller, Otterlo.

22: *Red Vineyards at Arles*, 1888, oil, 75 × 93 cm. Pushkin Museum, Moscow.

23: *The Dance Hall at Arles*, Dec 1888, oil, 65 × 81 cm. Musée d'Orsay, Paris.

25: *Garden in Provence*, July 1888, pen, 49 × 61 cm. Oskar Reinhart Collection, Winterthur.

26: *Memories of the North*, 1889, oil, State Museum Kröller-Müller, Otterlo.

27: *Street in Auvers*, 1890, oil, 73 × 92 cm. Kunstanyn Museum, Helsinki.

29: *Pollard Willows and Setting Sun*, October 1888, oil, 31.5 × 34.5 cm. State Museum Kröller-Müller, Otterlo.

30: *Thatched Cottages in Auvers*, July 1890, oil, 65 × 81 cm. Kunsthaus, Zurich.

31: *Meadow with Butterflies*, May 1890, oil, 64.5 × 91 cm. National Gallery, London.

32–33: *Entrance to the Public Gardens at Arles*, September 1888, oil, 72.5 × 91 cm. Phillips Collection, Washington, DC.

35: *St Paul's Hospital, Saint-Rémy*, 1889, oil, 58 × 45 cm. Musée d'Orsay, Paris.

37: *In the Orchard*, 1883, pen transfer lithograph, Christie's, London.

37: *Weaver: The Whole Loom*, March 1884, oil, Christie's, London.

37: *The Parsonage Garden in Winter*, 1885, Armand Hammer Foundation.

38: *Two Peasants Working in the Field*, April 1885, oil, 50 × 64 cm. Kunsthaus, Zurich.

38: *Bowl of Flowers*, 1886, oil, 50 × 61 cm. Stadtische Kunsthalle, Mannheim.

39: *Restaurant de la Sirène Asnières*, 1887, oil, 57 × 68 cm. Musée d'Orsay, Paris.

39: *Wheatfield with Lark*, June 1887, oil, 54 × 64.5 cm. National Museum Vincent Van Gogh, Amsterdam.

39: *Seascape at Sainte-Marie*, June 1888, oil, 44 × 53 cm. Pushkin Museum, Moscow.

40: *Boats with Men Unloading Sand*, August 1888, oil, 55 × 56 cm. Museum Folkwang, Essen.

40: *Binding the Sheaves*, 1889, oil, Stedelijk Museum, Amsterdam.

42: *Window of Vincent's Studio in the Asylum in St Rémy*, October 1889, black chalk, gouache, 61.5 × 47 cm. National Museum Vincent Van Gogh, Amsterdam.

SELECTED BIBLIOGRAPHY

Books:

DE LA FAILLE, J.-B., *The Works of Vincent Van Gogh*, Amsterdam, 1970.

HAMMACHER, A.M., *Van Gogh: A Documentary Biography*, London, 1982.

HULSKER, Jan, *The Complete Van Gogh: Paintings Drawings Sketches*, Amsterdam, 1978: Oxford and New York, 1980.

TRALBAUT, Marc, *Vincent Van Gogh*, London and New York, 1969.

VAN GOGH, Vincent, *The Complete Letters of Vincent Van Gogh*, 3 vols., introduction by V.W. Van Gogh, London and New York, 1958.

Exhibition catalogues:

English Influences on Vincent Van Gogh, Ronald Pickvance, London, 1974.

Van Gogh in Arles, Ronald Pickvance, Metropolitan Museum, New York, 1984.

Van Gogh in Saint-Rémy and Auvers, Ronald Pickvance, Metropolitan Museum, New York, 1986.

Van Gogh à Paris, Musée d'Orsay, Paris, 1988.

PHOTOGRAPH CREDITS